W9-ASZ-906

SCHOLARS, WRITERS, AND PROFESSIONALS

◆ ◆ ◆

AMERICAN INDIAN LIVES

SCHOLARS, WRITERS, AND PROFESSIONALS

◆ ◆ ◆

Jonathan W. Bolton
and Claire M. Wilson

Facts On File®

AN INFOBASE HOLDINGS COMPANY

On the cover: (left) N. Scott Momaday; (right) Susette La Flesche

Scholars, Writers, and Professionals

Copyright © 1994 by Jonathan W. Bolton and Claire M. Wilson

Facts On File, Inc.
460 Park Avenue South
New York NY 10016

Library of Congress Cataloging-in-Publication Data

Bolton, Jonathan William.
   Scholars, writers, and professionals / Jonathan W. Bolton and Claire M. Wilson.

      p. cm. — (American Indian lives)
   Includes bibliographical references and index.
   ISBN 0-8160-2896-6
      1. Indians of North America—Biography—Juvenile literature.
   [1. Indians of North America—Biography.]   I. Wilson, Claire.
   II. Title.   III. Series: American Indian lives (New York, N. Y.)
   E89.B65   1994
   920'.009297—dc20   93-31683

A British CIP catalogue record for this book is available from the British Library.

Facts On File books are available at special discounts when purchased in bulk quantities for businesses, associations, institutions or sales promotions. Please call our Special Sales Department in New York at 212/683-2244 or 800/322-8755.

Text design by Ellen Levine
Cover design by Nora Wertz
Composition by Grace M. Ferrara/Facts On File, Inc.
Manufactured by the Maple-Vail Book Manufacturing Group
Printed in the United States of America

10 9 8 7 6 5 4 3 2 1

This book is printed on acid-free paper.

For Polly

Parting is all we know of heaven,
And all we need of hell.
—Emily Dickinson

◆ ◆ ◆

CONTENTS

ACKNOWLEDGMENTS

◆ ◆ ◆

The authors wish to thank Nicole Bowen, for her editorial guidance and invaluable assistance; Sean Standing Bear of the Osage Tribal Museum in Pawhuska, Oklahoma; William H. Fenton; the staff of the McKeldin Library, University of Maryland; and Ruby.

INTRODUCTION

◆ ◆ ◆

Most of us enjoy reading about successful men and women to try to find out how they came to achieve greatness. Certain questions always arise: What were they like growing up? In what ways did they struggle? Did they ever think of giving up? What obstacles did they have to overcome? This book attempts to answer these questions. But it also has another purpose—to show that the answers to these questions are very different when we look at the success stories of Native Americans. In many cases, a Native American with ambition had to struggle against adversity in ways that other great men and women we read about did not.

Most of the Native Americans discussed in this book had to overcome racial prejudice and injustice, barriers of language and culture, limited education, poverty, and life-threatening diseases. And they each had unique challenges to face. Sequoyah set out late in his life to find the lost tribe of Cherokee and bring it back into the fold; John Rollin Ridge sought fortune during the gold rush of 1849, became embroiled in the California newspaper wars, and published alongside Mark Twain; Dr. Charles Eastman rode his horse through a blizzard to reach the dead and dying after hearing of the Wounded Knee massacre; Sarah Winnemucca sneaked into an enemy camp at night to rescue her aging father and lead him to safety.

This book begins with the story of Sequoyah, a Cherokee leader and the inventor of the Cherokee alphabet. But was he the first Native American scholar, writer, or professional? No, Native American literature did not begin with Sequoyah. Sequoyah's alphabet made it possible for his people to write their language and, therefore, record their songs, stories, and history, but prior to Sequoyah's invention, Native Americans had a long intellectual tradition—one that had been transmitted by word of mouth. In the Native American tradition, instead of seeking knowledge in books or formal schools, one would go to the tribal elders, or to one's grandmother. These people served as receptacles of wisdom and storehouses of myths, songs, rituals, and chants. In some ways, this oral tradition served the same purpose as books, in other ways it was different and unique. Stories and poems take on different meanings depending on who is telling them, and the facts change according to the art of each individual storyteller.

One of the writers discussed in this book, N. Scott Momaday, credits his grandmother and Kiowa tribal elders with a strong influence on his work. Authors Michael Dorris and Louise Erdrich, too, have said that they grew up hearing stories that had been passed on from generation to generation. Their way of telling stories by using a number of different narrators owes much to the Native American oral tradition. Because of this oral tradition, the stories, poems, and songs are remembered and retold while the teller is forgotten. Thus, there have been many Native American storytellers whose names will never be known.

In recognizing the achievements of the Native Americans who are known, we should keep in mind the many others who were responsible for preserving and transmitting their culture. Some of these preservers of culture are known by name and, in recognition of their important work, this book includes a chapter on Native American ethnographers. The ethnographers who recorded and preserved cultural artifacts—stories, myths, rituals, chants, and religious rites—have made it possible for us to acquire a greater understanding of Native American life and history. Without this valuable work, many aspects of tribal culture would have been lost forever. For most of the people occupied in this work, the responsibilities were tremendous.

For the three ethnologists discussed in this book—James Murie, Jesse Cornplanter, and John Joseph Mathews—their work was something of a labor of love, for it was the culture of their own people that they were trying to rescue. However, as with many other issues, the Indian community was often split in its feelings about ethnographers. Many Native Americans were opposed to the removal of sacred artifacts and objects from tribal lands, whether for sale to collectors or for preservation in museums. In addition, a number of non-Indian ethnologists and collectors swindled Indians out of valuable artifacts, sometimes even stealing them outright. Most Native American ethnologists usually worked with and were employed by non-Indians, and so had to contend with tribal members who accused them of "selling out" to the white man.

During the past two centuries, the traditional ways of Native Americans have been disappearing at a rapid pace. Much of this change can be attributed to U.S. government policy, especially the policy of assimilation, which is most clearly embodied in the Dawes Act of 1887. The Dawes Act was passed to make U.S. citizens of, and allot land to, all Native Americans. Although the act appeared to protect the Indians' rights to their land, it more often led to their being cheated out of or removed from sacred lands. Another purpose of the act was to assimilate Native Americans into the white world, which meant that they had to give up their traditional tribal customs, religion, language, and dress. In many cases, this policy turned Native Americans against themselves, dividing tribes into two groups: the traditionalists, who wished to retain the old way of life, and the progressives, who wanted to assimilate into the non-Indian world. Many of the writers and intellectuals discussed in this book had to come to terms with this issue of being "caught between two worlds."

This division persists to some degree even today. However, in the past 25 years there has been a strong movement among Native Americans to return to the traditional way of life. This movement would not have been possible had it not been for those who worked hard in the past to record these Native American traditions.

Although this is a book about Native American scholars, writers, and professionals, it is also a book about the Native American experience in general. The small group of scholars, writers, and professionals included in this book do not by any means represent the sum total of Native American intellectual achievement. As the transition from oral to print culture nears completion, the list of Native American writers continues to grow. In addition to Momaday, Erdrich, and Dorris, such talented poets and novelists as James Welch, Joy Harjo, Jim Barnes, Simon Ortiz, Leslie Marmon Silko, Martin Cruz Smith, Gerald Vizenor, and Paula Gunn Allen have emerged to form what has been called a Native American literary renaissance. This renaissance, or rebirth, can be seen as the fruit of the labors of earlier writers and professionals who struggled to achieve their goals in a world that refused to accept the Indian as an intellectual equal—a story that is repeated, in one form or another, in each of the lives discussed in this book.

SEQUOYAH
(GEORGE GUESS)

◆ ◆ ◆

Inventor of the Cherokee Syllabary
(c. 1770–1843)

Sometime around the winter of 1822, two great Cherokee leaders, Elias Boudinot and John Ross, were riding horseback through western Cherokee territory in what is today Oklahoma. Along the trail the two men passed a small cabin. Boudinot pointed out the cabin to Ross, saying disapprovingly that the man who lived there frittered away all of his time trying to invent a Cherokee alphabet. Boudinot and Ross continued on their journey and thought no more of the man and his work. But two years later, during a general council meeting of the Cherokee Nation, Boudinot saw a number of Western Cherokee writing and communicating information to one another in characters invented by one of their own people. Boudinot was astounded to learn that the inventor of this written language was Sequoyah, the man who had been laboring away in the very same cabin he and Ross had passed.

Boudinot was not the only man to have questioned Sequoyah's sanity. Most of Sequoyah's neighbors thought he was mad as well. The figures and characters that he scratched onto trees, slates, fences, and houses were thought by many to be spells or some form of witchcraft. Many of the Cherokee believed that written language or "talking leaves" were only available to white people.

Indeed, one Cherokee legend tells of how in the beginning of time, the Great Creator gave gifts to humans. To the Indians, he gave a book, to the white people he gave a bow and arrow. The Indians couldn't find any use for the book, but the white people wanted it. When the Indians neglected the book, the white people came and stole it. Thus the "talking leaves" were thought to be the sole province of the whites. But this attitude was to change, and within a short period of time, Sequoyah's image among his people, who had at one time been so opposed to his "talking leaves" that they burned down his house, went from that of a madman to that of a genius. And the work of this genius was to change Cherokee life and history.

◆ ◆ ◆

Little is known about Sequoyah's early life. It is generally believed that "Sikwa'yi," or George Guess, as he was known among the whites, was the son of a white man and a mixed-blood Cherokee woman. Some accounts of his parentage claim that his father was George Gist, a German trader who lived among the Cherokee in the 1760s. A more probable account claims that his father was Nathaniel Gist, who was captured by the Cherokee in 1755 and remained a prisoner for six years. It is thought that Sequoyah was born in 1770 and lived with his mother, Wurteh, near Tuskegee, in present-day Tennessee. He was the child of a distinguished family—his uncle was a Cherokee chief in the large settlement of Echota along the Tennessee River.

The mid-18th century was a difficult and turbulent period in which to start life. The Revolutionary War, fought by American colonists against their British rulers, had a profound effect on Cherokee life. The Cherokee Nation fought on the side of the British, and their warriors were embroiled in almost constant battle with American soldiers. Many Cherokee villages were attacked and burned to the ground by colonial armies. The population of Sequoyah's tribe was also diminishing, from the attacks of the American soldiers, from famine, and from epidemics.

Like many of his fellow tribesmen, Sequoyah was a hunter and a fur trader. Sometime during his young manhood, Sequoyah was injured in a hunting accident that left him with a debilitating physical handicap. In spite of this, he was also an expert silversmith, fashioning spoons and other utensils in the manner of the white blacksmiths. In addition to this skill, he was an excellent artist. Without ever having seen a paintbrush or paint, Sequoyah made brushes out of animal hair and made ink from the bark of trees.

During his young manhood Sequoyah had frequent contact with white civilization, and his curiosity was aroused by the way white people could "talk" to each other by making marks on paper. Although many Cherokee villages had been visited by Moravian and Catholic missionaries, Sequoyah was in his forties before his village received missionaries. Thus, he had never learned to speak, read, or write in English. In about 1809, despite the time consumed by all of his pursuits, Sequoyah first began working on a Cherokee alphabet.

For the Cherokee, the late 18th and early 19th centuries were especially troubled times. The Cherokee Nation was hit with a devastating earthquake in 1812, which resulted in many Cherokee relocating to the region between the Arkansas and White rivers. Hence, the Cherokee were split into Eastern and Western parts. And not only were the Cherokee deeply involved in the American Revolution, they were also continually battling with the hostile Creek Indians. Sequoyah had little choice but to fight for his life and for the life of his people. He was a soldier during the War of 1812 and fought alongside American soldiers against the Creek. In 1813, he was present at the liberation of Turkeytown, which had been taken over by the Creek. He also fought at the famous battle of Horseshoe Bend, which proved to be the decisive battle of the Creek and Cherokee war. Here, he was part of the reinforcement troop of 500 Cherokee from Tennessee that helped retreating General (later President) Andrew Jackson and his American militiamen turn back a huge army of Creek. The counterattack turned into a rout that left more than 800 Creek dead.

In 1817, Sequoyah was part of the delegation that signed a treaty with Andrew Jackson in which the Cherokee forfeited a large chunk of their land in exchange for territory west of the Mississippi River—a concession that would later cause great misery for the Cherokee Nation. After the treaty, many Cherokee voluntarily moved west. In 1818, Sequoyah and his wife, Sarah, whom he had married a few years earlier, were part of the second wave of Cherokee to settle in the West. Sequoyah worked on a longboat on the Arkansas River, helping Cherokee emigrants to relocate in their new land. Before the year was out, he built a log cabin in what is today Pope County, Arkansas, and settled down with his family.

With the end of the war, Sequoyah was able to return to his work on the alphabet. Although some versions of the story suggest that Sequoyah devised his alphabet at lightning-quick speed, most historians estimate that it took Sequoyah about 12 years to complete and perfect the Cherokee alphabet. Yet, considering the complexity of the Cherokee spoken language and the incredible difficulty of the task, even 12 years might be thought of as lightning-quick. Try to imagine being able to speak in a language without knowing how that language might look on the page. Imagine also that there is no one to teach you how to read or write because your language has never been written down. If you can imagine this, you have some idea of the problems that Sequoyah faced.

Using his skills as an artist, Sequoyah began by drawing pictographic symbols for each word in the Cherokee language—a system of writing that in some ways resembled ancient Greek and Egyptian modes of representing speech that took some 3,000 years to evolve. In all, Sequoyah came up with more than 1,000 pictures to match Cherokee words. However, knowing that it would be too hard to memorize these pictographs and draw them accurately, he abandoned this method. After three years of work, Sequoyah was back to the drawing board. He realized that spoken language consisted of a number of sounds or syllables that, when strung together, produced words and sentences carrying meaning. So he decided that it would be better to devise a symbol or picture to represent each sound made in Cherokee speech instead of each word. He and his daughter, who seems to have had an excellent ear for distinguishing the different

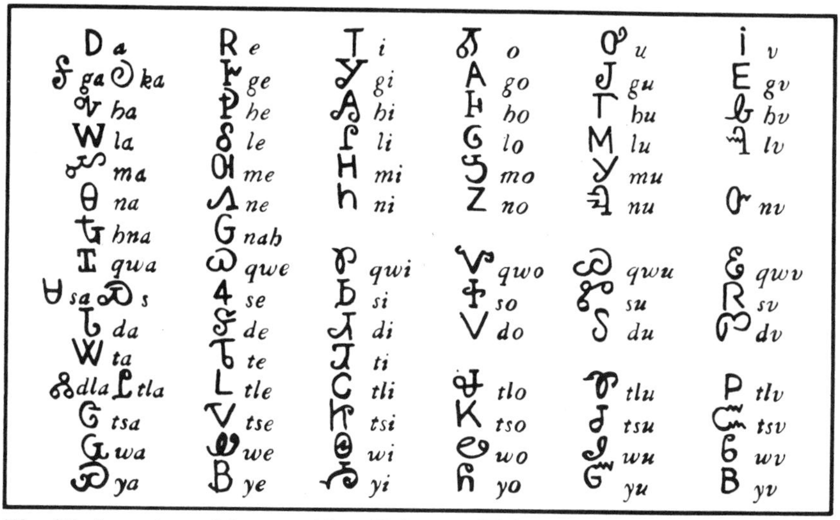

a	e	i	o	u	v
D a	R e	T i	δ o	O⁹ u	i v
S ga Ꮻ ka	✔ ge	Ꭹ gi	A go	J gu	E gv
ϑ ha	Ꮲ he	Ꭿ hi	Ᏺ ho	Ꭲ hu	ᴸ hv
W la	Ꮈ le	Ꮅ li	Ꮆ lo	M lu	Ꭿ lv
ᴔ ma	Ꮂ me	H mi	Ꮉ mo	Ꭶ mu	
θ na	Ꮑ ne	h ni	Z no	ᴧ nu	Ꮔ nv
Ꮕ hna	Ꮕ nah				
Ꮖ qua	ꙍ qwe	℘ qwi	ᏉＶ qwo	ꙮ qwu	Ꮗ qwv
Ꮄ sa ꙮ s	4 se	Ꮖ si	✝ so	ꙮ su	Ꮢ sv
Ꮣ da	Ꮥ de	Ꮧ di	V do	Ꮪ du	Ꮫ dv
Ꮃ ta	Ꮦ te	Ꮨ ti			
ꙮ dla Ꮮ tla	Ꮣ tle	C tli	Ꮊ tlo	Ꮖ tlu	P tlv
Ꮐ tsa	�v tse	Ᏺ tsi	K tso	Ꮳ tsu	Ꮲ tsv
Ꮹ wa	Ꮾ we	ꙮ wi	ꙮ wo	Ꮃ wu	6 wv
Ᏸ ya	Ꮽ ye	Ꮖ yi	ꭴ yo	Ꮆ yu	B yv

The 85 characters of Sequoyah's syllabary, which represent all of the sounds of the Cherokee language, enabled the Cherokee to produce their own "talking leaves." (Courtesy of the Sequoyah Birthplace Museum)

sounds of the Cherokee language, listened to and classified all of the syllables of their language.

Sequoyah classified a little more than 200 different syllables. He then matched these sounds to characters or letters, many of which were taken from the "talking leaves" of English-speaking people. Eventually Sequoyah narrowed the number of characters down to 85, and put them in a chart.

With the hard work of 12 years behind him and with the completion of his syllabary, there still remained a major problem for Sequoyah: except for himself and his children, no one knew how to read or write using his system. There was also the problem of convincing his people that he had really succeeded in learning how to make talking leaves. To say the least, Sequoyah's remarkable invention was greeted with no small amount of suspicion by his fellow Cherokee. But slowly he was able to convince others that he could really talk on paper. Having taught his daughter how to read and write using the syllabary, he arranged public demonstrations of his talking leaves. In these demonstrations, Sequoyah first sent his daughter out of hearing distance, then asked the observers to express something verbally. He would write this expression down on paper and send it to where his daughter was. His daughter then read this expression back exactly as it had been spoken.

Soon people began to believe that this was no mere magic trick. In 1821, leaders of the western branch of the Cherokee Nation put the syllabary to the ultimate test. Sequoyah was ordered to teach his syllabary to a few of the sons of important Cherokee men. After only two months of instruction, Sequoyah had taught them how to read and write in Cherokee. Not only did the syllabary work, it was easy to learn. It is generally believed that by 1823, through the use of Sequoyah's invention, at least 1,000 Cherokee had learned to read and write in their own language. Whole villages were transformed into academies for the learning of the syllabary. Letters and messages were sent back and forth between Cherokee in the West and those back East. The two halves of the Cherokee Nation, separated by nearly 500 miles, were being unified through the help of Sequoyah's invention.

Sequoyah was finally recognized as a man of great genius. American newspapers in the East told of his remarkable invention and began calling him the Indian "Cadmus," likening Sequoyah to the legendary inventor of the Greek alphabet. In 1824, the legislative council of the Cherokee Nation presented him with a medal in gratitude for the great gift that he had bestowed on his people. And within a short period of time, Sequoyah's invention began to have an increasing influence on Cherokee life. For years missionaries had been struggling with the barriers of language. Up to this time they had been forced to communicate their religious messages via translators. That is, Cherokee who had adopted the Christian religion, be it Catholicism, Moravianism, or Baptism, had to learn English in order to read from the Bible. With the invention of a written Cherokee language, missionaries saw an opportunity to translate the Bible into Cherokee, thereby increasing the number of converts and enhancing the understanding of those already converted.

First, a Moravian convert named Atsi and a native Cherokee translated part of the Gospel of John and distributed copies of their translation throughout the Cherokee Nation. In 1825, a mixed-blood preacher named David Brown completed a manuscript translation of the New Testament. In 1827, Samuel Worcester, a missionary from Boston, convinced the American Board of Missions to finance the manufacture of a printing press using the characters from Sequoyah's syllabary. This led to the creation of the *Cherokee Phoenix*—a newspaper printed in both English and Cherokee. The editor of this paper was none other than Elias Boudinot.

With the successful institution of the Cherokee printing press, Cherokee leaders could now draw up, print, and circulate a tribal constitution. This was accomplished in 1827 at New Echota, Georgia. As this demonstrates, the effects of Sequoyah's invention were far-reaching. It enabled his people to progress, helping them to achieve an ever-increasing pride in themselves and in their culture. The Cherokee had always thought of themselves as a nation among other nations; now they felt they had justified that claim.

The pride that the Cherokee took in being able to read and write was enormous. But this pride was soon to suffer a severe blow—in 1829 the state of Georgia, backed by President Andrew Jackson, gave the Cherokee the option of either giving up their land in the East, moving to the West, and retaining their tribal identities, or of remaining in the East, becoming U.S. citizens, and accepting allotments of land. In 1830 Jackson pushed the Indian Removal Act through Congress. The circumstances that led to this event are complicated, but the basic cause of the removal was the discovery of gold on Cherokee land. White prospectors had been invading Cherokee lands since 1815, erecting mining camps and building small villages, and the Georgia militia backed up the claims of these prospectors with force. Many Cherokee were bullied into moving west, but many others stayed to fight it out. These unfortunate people were later forcibly removed. Unprepared for the long and arduous journey westward, and deprived of necessary supplies and means of travel, thousands of Cherokee died along what has come to be called the "Trail of Tears."

In 1832, the Cherokee printing press in the offices of the *Cherokee Phoenix* was silenced by the state of Georgia. Although the U.S. government had applauded the genius of Sequoyah's invention, it now saw that this same invention could be used to stir up trouble by telling the world about the government's inexcusable treatment of the Cherokee. The syllabary was now seen as a threat to white authority. In fact, the U.S. government later reneged on a promise of $1,000 to the Cherokee that was to be used for building another printing press in the West.

The surviving Eastern Cherokee joined their fellow tribe members west of the Mississippi River. Although the nation was unified in a geographical sense for the first time since 1812, in other ways it was in a shambles. In 1829 Sequoyah had moved to Indian Territory near Sallisaw in present-day Sequoyah, Oklahoma. Now Sequoyah, a much-respected leader of the Western Cherokee, teamed with Eastern Cherokee leaders John Ross and George Lowrey in reconstructing the nation. At first, leaders of the western branch were unwilling to meet with the leaders of the eastern branch. But through the help of Sequoyah and his influence over the "old settlers" of the western branch, a meeting was finally arranged. Sequoyah, always pleased to have a chance to communicate via "talking leaves," was instrumental in bringing the two factions together:

> We, the old settlers, are here in council with the late emigrants, and we want you to come up without delay, that we may talk matters over like friends and brothers. These people are here in great multitudes, and they are perfectly friendly towards us. . . . We send you these few lines as friends and we want you to come without delay; and we have no doubt but we can have all things amicably and satisfactorily settled.

And things *were* somewhat amicably settled. The tribal leaders agreed upon a new constitution in 1839, and the Cherokee Nation was finally unified under one set of laws and one form of government.

The only depiction of Sequoyah painted from life that has come down to us is by artist Charles Bird King, who painted Sequoyah in 1828 during his visit to Washington, D.C. as part of a delegation of Western Cherokee. The portrait seems to capture the thoughtful, philosophical nature of the man. As his fame spread,

SE - QUO-YAH

In Charles Bird King's famous painting of 1828, Sequoyah is shown pointing to the final version of the Cherokee syllabary. (Courtesy of the Sequoyah Birthplace Museum)

Sequoyah had many visitors to his cabin. Many descriptions of him by these visitors survive. One such description, provided by the distinguished scholar of American literature Samuel Lorenzo Knapp, is a typical characterization of Sequoyah:

No stoic could have been more grave in his demeanour than was See-quah-ya; he pondered, according to the Indian custom, for a considerable time after each question was put, before making his reply, and often took a whiff of his calumet [pipe] while reflecting on an answer.

Another account of a meeting with Sequoyah comes from Philadelphia merchant John Alexander:

He is of pleasant countenance and indicates a good deal of genius. He conversed freely on various topics, becoming very animated when my answers & questions pleased him.

By the time the Cherokee Nation was being reconstructed in the West, Sequoyah was more than 70 years old. He had seen his syllabary adopted as the official written language of his people. He had also witnessed the hardships and near dissolution of the Cherokee. Yet he was far from being weary of this world, and he did not consider his work finished. In 1842, Sequoyah and a group of Cherokee companions visited the villages of Indian tribes to the southwest in order to examine their language. It is generally believed that Sequoyah was thinking about devising a universal Indian alphabet, one that would allow all American Indians to communicate among themselves. But if this was in fact his intention, nothing ever came of it.

In 1843, Sequoyah went in search of a tribe of "lost" Cherokee who, it was thought, had settled somewhere in northern Mexico. It was Sequoyah's desire to spread word of his syllabary to this remote tribe, teach them how to use the syllabary, and restore communication between them and the Cherokee Nation. For a short period Sequoyah and his search party lived among the Wichita Indians. From the Wichita they learned that there was a village of Cherokee somewhere along the Washita River. As they were readying themselves to travel there, Sequoyah began to suffer from a pain in his chest. Eager to find the Cherokee village, Sequoyah did not think it necessary to rest and regain his health. After two weeks of travel, his condition began to worsen. Still they pushed on, finally reaching the river mentioned by the Wichita. They set up camp near the Mexican village of San Fernando, but by this time Sequoyah was too ill to travel further. Part of the group went off in search of the village, and the rest remained to look after Sequoyah. The search party did locate the Cherokee village—but sadly, when they returned to camp, after about two weeks, they found that Sequoyah had died.

News of Sequoyah's death spread quickly through the Cherokee Nation. Nearly every Cherokee paused to reflect on the life of this great man and the gift of a written language that he had bestowed on them. The *Cherokee Advocate,* a Cherokee newspaper that is still published today, recommended that the Cherokee Nation honor Sequoyah's memory by giving a pension to his widow. This pension was just the first of many gestures honoring his life. In 1851 the Cherokee council voted to rename the Skin Bayou region the Sequoyah District, and this later became Sequoyah County when Oklahoma was admitted to the Union in 1907. In 1911, the state of Oklahoma commissioned a statue of Sequoyah and placed it in the State Capitol building. In 1936 the cabin where Sequoyah had lived from 1829 on was made a national landmark, and the surrounding village also took on his name. His birthplace in Vonore, Tennessee was also made a national landmark some years later. There is a monument to Sequoyah in Calhoun, Georgia, which is near the former Cherokee capital, New Echota. And the giant redwood trees of California, called Sequoia, were named for the man who used to scratch his pictographs on the barks of trees. But perhaps the most fitting tribute came, ironically, from Alexander Posey, a poet of the Creek Nation, traditional enemies of the Cherokee:

> The people's language cannot perish—nay,
> When from the face of this great continent
> Inevitable doom hath swept away
> The last memorial—the last fragment
> Of tribes,—some scholar learned shall pore
> Upon thy letters, seeking lore.
> Some bard shall lift a voice in praise of thee,
> In moving numbers tell the world how men
> Scoffed thee, hissed thee, charged with lunacy!
> And who could not give 'nough honor when
> At length, in spite of jeers, of want and need,
> Thy genius shaped a dream into a deed.

JOHN ROLLIN RIDGE

◆ ◆ ◆

Cherokee Poet, Novelist, Journalist, and Historian (1827–67)

On June 22, 1839, a young John Rollin Ridge was roused from sleep by gunshots. He ran downstairs and out the front door and saw three men dragging his father, John Ridge, across the yard. His father struggled fiercely to free himself, but finally he was subdued, and as young John watched, the men plunged their knives into Ridge's body. Then they fled to the woods, where horses were awaiting them, and disappeared into the early morning mist. For the Ridge family, the tragedy did not end there. About 30 miles away another group of assassins came upon John Rollin Ridge's grandfather, Major Ridge, on the road, and fired five bullets into his chest. He was found dead a few hours later. It was eventually discovered that the killings had been planned by supporters of the Ridges' political rival, John Ross, including Ross's son, Allen. Ridge later wrote that the sight of his father's assassination "darkened [his] mind with an eternal shadow." Indeed, he would go through life always bearing a grudge against John Ross and his supporters.

◆ ◆ ◆

John Rollin Ridge was born into an illustrious half-blooded Cherokee family on March 19, 1827, near present-day Rome,

Georgia, at the southern edge of traditional Cherokee territory. His grandfather, Major Ridge (also known as "The Ridge"), had distinguished himself in the wars against the Creek Nation in 1812. Major Ridge later became the leader of a Cherokee movement that called for increased education, the revision of laws that governed tribal membership, and the assimilation of Cherokee into the "white man's world." Ridge's father, John Ridge, a lawyer and prosperous farmer, joined his father's cause.

The wealth and eminence of the Ridge family gave John Rollin Ridge advantages that were not available to most Cherokee children of the time. He had his own private tutor, had 419 acres of land to roam in, and lived comfortably in a large, two-story house. But as the son and grandson of political leaders in a turbulent period in Cherokee history, John Rollin Ridge also learned at an early age that life could be dangerous.

The Ridge family's troubles began almost as soon as Andrew Jackson became president in 1829. After his election, Jackson announced a plan to remove all Indians east of the Mississippi to territory in the West in response to pressure from white settlers. The state of Georgia, too, made clear its intentions to take over all Cherokee land within its borders. But the Cherokee were not about to give up without a fight.

John Ridge and his friend Elias Boudinot took a peaceful approach to the problem by speaking to groups in New York, Boston, and Philadelphia to win support for the Cherokee cause. They also traveled to Washington, D.C., to protest Jackson's decree before the U.S. Supreme Court. Although they succeeded in getting the Supreme Court to declare Indian removal unconstitutional, the court's decision was never enforced. Under Jackson's orders, federal officials simply refused to protect the Indians' right to keep their land.

After nearly two years of witnessing violence and living in fear, the Ridges and other Cherokee leaders decided that resistance was useless. In 1835, a group of 20 Cherokee leaders, led by John and Major Ridge, made an agreement to give up all of their land in the East in exchange for 13 million acres of land in the West. Although many Cherokee packed up and moved west after the treaty was signed, others refused to leave. As a result, in 1838 the Georgia militia began to remove the remaining Cherokee by force. So began one of the saddest events in Native American history, an event that became known as the "Trail of Tears." In the dead of winter, thousands of Cherokee of all ages were herded across hundreds of miles of inhospitable territory with meager supplies. Some died of exposure and sickness, some drowned when they were forced to cross rivers in unseaworthy boats, and many more died of starvation. By the time the last group reached the West, the death toll was nearly 4,000, approximately one-fifth of the Cherokee population.

The Ridge family, however, did not suffer because of the deal that Major and John Ridge had made. They had resettled a year earlier in a region of Missouri known as Honey Creek. By the time most Cherokee reached the new territory, John Ridge had cleared a section of good farmland and opened a store. Not surprisingly, the ease of John Ridge's resettlement, when compared to the suffering of the Cherokee who had taken the Trail of Tears, was a source of deep resentment. In addition, John Ross and John Howard Payne, leaders of the Cherokee who had opposed land exchange, blamed the Ridges for all the Cherokee troubles. Ross's first wife, Quatie, had been among those who died on the Trail of Tears.

After the murders of John and Major Ridge in Honey Creek, John Rollin Ridge's mother, Sarah, moved the family to Fayetteville, Arkansas, to protect them from further violence. Here, removed from the dangers of Cherokee infighting, Ridge grew up in relative peace and calm. His formal education began at Mount Comfort School, where he first fell in love with literature. Ridge's favorite authors were the British poets Lord Byron and John Keats—influences that would later affect his own poetry.

In 1845, Ridge also began a course of study that he hoped would help him in his other interest—restoring his family fortune, which had been lost when they fled Honey Creek. He began studying law in preparation for setting up a successful practice. As it turned out, however, the family fortune was restored without Ridge having to do anything. In 1847, President James K. Polk approved a Cherokee treaty that had as one of its provisions, in reparation for loss of land and money, a payment of $5,000 to the estate of John Ridge.

That same year, Ridge married Elizabeth Wilson, and the feud between the Ridge and Ross factions had quieted down enough for Ridge to return with his wife to Honey Creek. No longer worried about money, Ridge decided to focus his attention on writing. During the next two years, he published several poems in Arkansas and Texas newspapers under the name Yellow Bird—an English translation of his Cherokee name, *Chees-quat-a-law-ny*. But his quiet literary life did not last.

One day in 1849 Ridge discovered that one of his horses was missing. A few days later he spotted the horse on a farm owned by his neighbor David Kell, who happened to be one of John Ross's friends. Ridge went to get his horse back, an argument erupted, and Kell approached Ridge as if to strike him. Ridge pulled out a gun and shot Kell dead. And although Ridge believed that he had killed Kell in self-defense, he feared that others would not see it that way. Again, Ridge was forced to flee the Cherokee Nation.

In that year of 1849, gold had just been discovered in California. Like thousands of men eager to strike it rich, Ridge saw an opportunity to increase his family's fortunes. He and his brother, Aeneas, pooled their resources and bought horses, mules, mining tools, and a carriage, and joined a wagon train heading west. Travel was difficult. They had to cross rivers, mountains, and deserts, and the burden of the supplies was often too much to carry. Ridge and his party had to abandon their wagons and many of their supplies, keeping only essentials. (Later, in California, they were forced to replace these supplies at 10 times the original cost.)

By the time the Ridge brothers reached California, they had spent most of their money. To make matters worse, there was no place to dig for gold—all the claims had been taken. Ridge eventually teamed up with a group of miners from Arkansas and began mining in an area called Whiskey Creek. But at best, he earned only four or five dollars a day, and most of that went for room and board. Food and tools were in short supply and were very expensive. Mining was backbreaking work and it seldom paid off—very few miners actually struck it rich. Ridge was not to be one of them.

After a few months of mining, Ridge had to face facts: he was not going to get rich as a miner. Like many other failed miners,

Ridge wound up looking for a job. He began his search in Sacramento, and had his first stroke of luck since leaving Honey Creek. He wrote an article about the hardships he had experienced on his journey to California and submitted it to the local agent for *True Delta*, a New Orleans–based newspaper. The agent for the paper was amazed at the quality of the writing, and he not only promised to publish the article but hired Ridge on the spot. Ridge became the news agent and correspondent of *True Delta* for the Yuba City/Marysville region of California.

In addition to writing articles, Ridge stepped up his literary production. During the early 1850s, again writing under the name Yellow Bird, he was a major contributor to *The Golden Era*, a popular literary journal that published work by such great writers as Bret Harte and Mark Twain. "Yellow Bird"'s poetry also found its way into well-known periodicals such as *Alta California, Hesperion*, and *Hutching's California Magazine*.

In his writing, Ridge showed that he had not forgotten his Cherokee heritage. For instance, in "Cherokee Love Song," Ridge fondly recalled his early life among the Cherokee and praised the beauty of Cherokee women. His poetry also displayed his broad knowledge of English literature and his ability to adapt that tradition to his own thoughts and feelings.

Writing poetry, however, was no way to earn a living, so Ridge turned his talents to popular fiction. In 1854, he published *The Life and Adventures of Joaquin Murieta,* a novel that told of the exploits of a real-life character named Joaquin Murieta—a legendary Western outlaw who, after years of evading the authorities, had been caught and beheaded a year earlier. Ridge presented an accurate and sympathetic portrayal of Murieta, and his research was so thorough that for years historians accepted his account of Murieta's life as factual. But, as certain passages show, Ridge was inclined to add to the Murieta legend and to sensationalize the outlaw's life. For example, in describing one of Murieta's brushes with the California rangers, Ridge writes:

> "I am Joaquin Murieta! Kill me if you can!"
> Shot after shot came clanging around his head, and bullet after

bullet flattened on the wall of slate at his right. In the midst of the first firing, his hat was knocked from his head, and left his long black hair streaming behind him. He had no time to use his own pistol, but, knowing that his only chance lay in the swiftness of his sure-footed animal, he drew his keenly polished bowie knife in proud defiance of the danger and waved it in scorn as he rode on.

It is easy to see why Ridge, like many other Californians of the period, found the bandit so appealing. He was an underdog who, when treated unfairly and cheated out of what belonged to him, fought back. Murieta was a Mexican-American who, like Ridge, had gone to California in search of gold. But the state of California passed a law that made it illegal for foreigners (mostly Mexicans) to mine for gold. This law was later changed so that foreigners could mine, but they had to pay a tax of $20 a month to do so. With only a limited amount of gold to go around, violence against Mexican miners by whites was common. Murieta was a victim of such an attack, in which he was tied to a tree and badly beaten. Rather than give in to this terrorism, he joined with other Mexicans who wanted to fight back, and eventually became their leader. Ridge, who had seen his people cheated in a similar way, seemed to identify strongly with Murieta.

The novel was very popular in California, Mexico, and Central America, and it was well received by critics. One reviewer said that Ridge's novel "[was] an argument in favor of Indian capacity." Although this sounds condescending today, many white Americans of the time did not believe that an Indian was capable of writing anything, let alone a novel. Although the publication of *Joaquin Murieta* made Ridge a well-known writer, it did not make him rich. Other accounts of Murieta's story appeared soon afterward, many of them borrowing extensively from Ridge's novel, and as a result his book sold poorly. (There was little copyright protection for authors in those days.)

By that time, however, Ridge had become a well-respected journalist, and job offers soon came his way. In 1855, General James Allen, a prominent California politician, founded a newspaper called the *California American* and hired Ridge as the paper's chief writer. However, Allen was a leader in the conservative Know-

Nothing party—a party whose members proclaimed themselves "protectors of the constitution" while at the same time promoting strict immigration laws to keep out Irish Catholics and opposing the movement to outlaw slavery—and the paper more and more became the official publication of the party. Ridge often disagreed with the views presented by other writers for the *California American* and came to dislike the paper's political affiliation.

In 1857 Ridge teamed up with fellow editor S. J. May to found the *Sacramento Daily Bee.* In the editorial column of the first issue, Ridge promised readers a newspaper free of political influence. This was rare indeed in an era when many newspapers were mouthpieces for a political party. The *Bee* also gave Ridge the opportunity to voice his own opinions. Remembering his experiences in the gold mines, Ridge became a defender of workers' rights. He also became an outspoken advocate of Manifest Destiny—the belief that the United States government was destined, by the will of God, to "civilize," Christianize, and rule the entire continent of North America. Ridge was not immune to the prejudices of his time. As a supporter of the separation of church and state, Ridge in his columns frequently attacked the Mormons, who had in the 1850s been granted religious freedom in Utah. Oddly, Ridge also argued in favor of slavery in California. The country was being rocked and divided by a series of difficult issues during those years, and Ridge's voice was one of many that shaped the public opinion of the day.

In late 1857, the ever-restless Ridge sold his interest in the *Daily Bee* and moved on to other things. He was hired as editor-in-chief of a new paper in Marysville called the *Daily National Democrat.* At this time, Ridge's wife, Elizabeth, and his nine-year-old daughter, Alice, finally joined him in California. The two weren't in California long before they got a true sense of the fame and popularity that Ridge had attained. A festival was held to honor the laying of a cable across the Atlantic Ocean that would connect telegraph lines between the United States and England, and Ridge was asked to read a commemorative poem at the celebration. Known to the people of Marysville as the author of *Joaquin Murieta*, Ridge began the festivities by reading his "Poem on the Atlantic Cable," a work that celebrated the progress of humanity.

> Let all mankind rejoice! for time nor space
> Shall check the progress of the human race!
> Though Nature heaved the Continents apart,
> She cast in one great mould the human heart.

The words reflected Ridge's belief that the history of humanity was one of evolutionary progress, and that society was forever advancing toward perfection. Ridge must have been a great success at the festival, for the following year he was asked to be the featured speaker at Marysville's Fourth of July celebration.

Although Ridge wrote about many of the controversial issues of his day, by the late 1850s one issue became important above all others—the controversy over slavery. The Democratic party, with which Ridge sympathized, was against the abolition of slavery—mainly because they felt it would divide the country and because they did not want to lose the political support of the Southern states. Ridge believed that the Democratic Illinois senatorial candidate in 1858, Stephen A. Douglas, would help to keep the country unified. Douglas's opponent in the election, the Republican party's candidate, was a lawyer from Illinois named Abraham Lincoln. Although they were running in a state election, the debates between Douglas and Lincoln concerned issues of national importance and drew the interest of the entire nation. Douglas argued that it was up to the individual states to decide whether slavery should be legal or not, while Lincoln, who felt that slavery should eventually be abolished, argued that slavery should not be allowed to spread to other states and territories. Lincoln lost the Senate seat to Douglas, but defeated Douglas in the presidential election two years later.

Ridge threw himself into the fight, becoming a prominent figure in the California Democratic party. In his editorials, Ridge championed Douglas, and, though he was against secession (slave states declaring their independence from the United States), he printed a speech in the *California Democrat* by Jefferson Davis, leader of the Southern states, announcing that the South would break away from the Union if Lincoln were elected president.

When Lincoln became president in 1860, Ridge wasted no time in taking up another cause—at least temporarily. This time he came out on the side of human rights. Ridge used his editorial column to protest the state government's treatment of the Yuba Indians, who were being removed from their land and forced onto a reservation. Like his father and grandfather before him, Ridge felt that all Indians should be assimilated into society, not shuffled off and penned up like cattle. Ridge also recommended the establishment of a separate Indian state, one in which Indians would be given good land and be allowed to govern themselves. While this may seem contradictory, Ridge argued that this could be done without alienating the Indians from American society at large.

In keeping with his interest in the Yuba Indians and in his own tribe, the Cherokee, Ridge published a number of essays on Indian history, mythology, religion, and customs. Many of these articles demonstrate that Ridge was familiar with the most advanced methods of his day in the fields of ethnology (the study of cultures) and anthropology (the study of human beings). He felt that the main problem with Indian relations and policy was that most Americans were ignorant of Indian ways, and through his essays, he hoped to win new respect for Indian culture and history.

In May 1861, Ridge became editor of the San Francisco *National Herald*—an anti-Lincoln, anti-abolitionist newspaper. Upon Ridge's arrival, a rival paper had this to say about the *Herald's* new editor:

> His editorial articles are always terse, perspicuous, free from prejudice and clothed in elegant English. He is a poet of no mean pretensions. His verses on "Mount Shasta" have a widespread popularity, and may be justly classed amongst the brilliant gems of the more celebrated of American poets.

At the *Herald*, Ridge was given his own column, "Topics of the Day." Later that year, Ridge was named the Democratic party's candidate for state printer—the highest honor a journalist could achieve in California. But he lost to the Republican candidate. The

Civil War had begun in early 1861, and, at this point in history, everything was split along the lines of Republican and Democrat, abolitionist and anti-abolitionist, North and South.

In 1862, President Lincoln drew up the preliminary version of the Emancipation Proclamation, declaring the end of slavery in the United States (the final version would be enacted January 1, 1863). With more and more citizens of California throwing their support behind Lincoln, Ridge's anti-Lincoln editorials were becoming less tolerable. His popularity began to fall off, as did the circulation of most Democratic newspapers. And as the fortunes of the Democratic party began to decline, so did those of John Rollin Ridge.

In 1863, Ridge relocated with his family to Grassville, California, to become editor of the Grassville *National*, another Democratic paper. In Grassville, a feud soon developed between the *National* and the Republican paper, *The Nevada Daily Gazette*. By now the Civil War was well under way, and these two newspapers were engaged in their own version of it. Ridge was accused by the *Gazette* of recruiting soldiers for the South, and the paper also argued that, because Ridge was a half-blooded Cherokee, he had no legal right to vote (Indians were not yet U.S. citizens). Never one to back down from a fight, Ridge countered with his own accusations and insults. On three occasions during the Civil War years, Ridge either challenged a rival editor or was challenged by a rival editor to a duel. In the late 19th century, "newspaper wars" were sometimes, quite literally, wars, so Ridge's quarrelsome behavior was not unusual; nevertheless, his opinionated writings during this period did a great deal of harm to his once-solid reputation as a fair, objective, and reliable journalist.

During the Civil War, the Cherokee Nation, like the United States, was divided between North and South. Cherokees fought on both sides. As a result, when the war was over in 1865, the Cherokee Nation faced some of the same difficulties during the Reconstruction period that the United States as a whole did. And Ridge, whose fame as a politician, poet, and journalist was as great among the Cherokee as it was among the general population of California, became a major figure in the efforts to heal the division in the Cherokee Nation. In February 1866, when a Cherokee delegation to Washington was

Ridge (far left) was a member of the Cherokee delegation to Washington in 1866. Members included (from left to right) Ridge, Saladin Watie, Richard Fields, Elias Boudinot, and William Penn Adair. (Photo by Alexander Gardner; Courtesy of the Archives and Manuscripts Division of the Oklahoma Historical Society)

organized, Ridge was asked to be the group's leader. The delegation's meetings with Congress led to the partitioning of the Cherokee Nation, and Ridge played an important part in this decision. It was his position that followers of John Ross would be too powerful if the Cherokee Nation remained unified. As part of his argument, Ridge recalled the assassinations of his father and grandfather, and appealed to the government to divide the Cherokee so as to avoid similar tragedies. Ridge and his fellow delegates were able to convince the government of the necessity for partition. It was a major victory for Ridge over his long-time enemy, John Ross.

Ridge returned to California in 1866 and resumed his duties as editor and writer. The newspaper wars of the 1850s and 1860s had subsided. But Ridge continued to attack the Republicans—this time for their Reconstruction policies.

In early 1867, Ridge's health began to deteriorate, and he

suffered severe headaches, dizziness, and fatigue. On October 5, 1867, Ridge died.

The California newspapers, in recognition of one their state's greatest journalists, praised the life and career of John Rollin Ridge. Ridge was also eulogized as a talented poet and as the writer of *Joaquin Murieta*.

Ridge's reputation as one of the first great Native American writers has survived. His poems were published shortly after his death, his novel *Joaquin Murieta* was reissued in 1986, and his essays on American Indian culture were the subject of a study in 1981. During the course of his long writing career, Ridge became famous for the outspoken and passionate manner in which he addressed the most important issues of his day. Above all, Ridge knew the power of the pen, and realized that literature provided a medium through which the Native American voice could be heard—a voice that was too seldom heard during his lifetime.

SARAH WINNEMUCCA

◆ ◆ ◆

Paiute Educator, Writer, Interpreter, and Activist (1844–91)

> *My people have no learning. They do not know anything about the history of the world, but they can see the Spirit-Father in everything. The beautiful world talks to them of their Spirit-Father. They are innocent and simple, but they are brave and will not be imposed upon. They are patient, but they know black is not white.*
>
> —Sarah Winnemucca, *Life Among the Piutes: Their Wrongs and Claims* (1883)

This passage, taken from Sarah Winnemucca's autobiography, tells us as much about her as it does about her people. She had very little formal education and knew nothing of the history of the world. She was brave—many times she put her life in danger in order to help her people—and she "would not be imposed upon." Whenever a government agent, politician, military officer, or journalist committed an injustice against the Paiute, they found themselves up against a formidable opponent in Sarah Winnemucca. Her life was a long battle against the forces that sought to cheat the Paiute out of their land and livelihood. Her eloquent speeches and passionate letters drew attention to the plight of her people and helped to achieve reform on Paiute reservations. At a time when whole tribes were being exterminated, either through war, starvation, or disease, the support won through Winnemucca's efforts saved countless numbers of Northern Paiute from a similar fate.

◆ ◆ ◆

Little is known about the early life of Sarah Winnemucca, other than that she was born near Humboldt Lake, Nevada, in 1844. She was given the name Thocmectony, meaning "shell flower." Her mother, Tuboitonie, carried Sarah on her back as she roamed through the forest gathering pine nuts, a staple food in the Paiute diet. Her father, Old Winnemucca, was an antelope shaman, not so much a healer as one who led the communal antelope hunts. Old Winnemucca later became chief of the Northern Paiute, although his right to that title was disputed by rebel bands.

At the age of six, Sarah was taken by her maternal grandfather, Truckee, to live in California. They settled just outside Stockton, where Sarah first came into contact with the white world. This contact became more intimate when Sarah was sent with her brothers, Natchez and Tom, to work on a ranch north of Stockton along the San Joaquin River. There were a number of Mexicans on the ranch as well, some of whom were married to Paiute women, and through these workers Sarah learned to speak Spanish. She later learned to speak English as well when she became the housekeeper for a woman in Stockton.

In 1857, Sarah and her sister Elma became housekeepers for the family of Major William M. Ormsby in Genoa, Nevada. Up to this time, Sarah had been treated with kindness and generosity by the white people she met, but at Genoa, she witnessed an event that would change all that. Two white traders had been found dead, with Indian arrows stuck in their bodies. The arrows were discovered to be those of the Washo Indians. The chief of the Washo was summoned by the sheriff of Genoa and was told to bring in the guilty Indians. The chief returned the next day with four men, all of whom denied that they had had any part in the death of the traders. Sarah watched as the four men, still pleading innocence, were shot and killed. A week later it was discovered that the actual murderers were two white men, and that they had used the Washo arrows to make it look as though Indians had committed the crime.

In 1858, Winnemucca accompanied the Ormsby family when they moved to Carson City, where Major Ormsby opened a hotel and general store, taking advantage of the booming town's growing population. Early the following year, silver was discovered in Carson City. Prospectors from California flocked to the town, and Major Ormsby's business thrived. The silver rush was not a good thing, however, for the Paiute, whose reservation life was seriously threatened—prospectors moved onto their land and staked claims.

It was not long before the new settlers discovered that the Paiute "would not be imposed upon," to use Winnemucca's words. In the winter of 1859, a white prospector was murdered and his property stolen by a band of Smoke Creek Paiute—a group that had broken from Old Winnemucca's control. When white representatives approached the Smoke Creek Paiute to request that the murderers be handed over, they were taken prisoner. Later on, two white settlers were found dead. Although these incidents were spread out over time and not part of a pattern, the press and agents of the U.S. Indian Bureau declared that Nevada had a full-scale Indian uprising on its hands.

That year, Major Ormsby led a troop of about 100 volunteers against the Smoke Creek Paiute, who had set up camp to the north of Carson City at Pyramid Lake. Ormsby and the volunteers soon learned something about Paiute military strategy. They walked right into a trap and were surrounded by Paiute; nearly 80 of the volunteers were killed, among them Major Ormsby. This incident became known as the Pyramid Lake War, and the government's response to the volunteers' defeat was swift but peaceful. It established a fort to protect Carson City and made arrangements to create a reservation for the Paiute. Although the idea of a reservation has come to mean isolation and the limitation of personal freedom, the Paiute at that time took it to mean that they could have their own land and could go on with their traditional life without fear of white interference.

During this troubled time, Sarah and Elma had returned to live with Old Winnemucca. But when the troubles had passed, they were once again sent off to live among white people. It is apparent that Old Winnemucca, knowing the value of fluency in the English language, encouraged the girls to become familiar with white culture. He especially wanted Sarah to become an interpreter—white interpreters could not always be trusted, and Indian interpreters often knew very little English. Thus the sisters were enrolled in the Notre Dame convent school in San Jose, California. It was here that Sarah got her first lesson in racial prejudice. She describes the experience in *Life Among the Piutes:*

> We were [at Notre Dame] only a few weeks, when complaints were made to the sisters by wealthy parents about Indians being in school with their children. The sisters then wrote to our friends to come and take us away, and so they did.

Sarah did, nevertheless, manage to get an education. What she lacked in formal education, she made up for by teaching herself. It is a testament to her intelligence and perseverence that she could learn a language so remote from her own. And not only did she learn to speak English, she also became highly skilled at writing in English, as anyone who reads *Life Among the Piutes* can see.

When Sarah and Elma rejoined Old Winnemucca at Pyramid Lake, where the Paiute reservation had been established, they found their people settling into a relatively untroubled way of life. The new governor of the Nevada territory, James Nye, had taken measures to remove white settlers from fertile land that belonged to the Paiute. It appeared that they had at last found someone who would uphold their rights. However, a toll road was built across the southern end of the reservation. As it turned out, this road was the beginning of more trouble for the Paiute. Likewise, the Paiute, who hunted for much of their food, often pursued game outside the boundaries of the reservation. The Nevada government considered this a sign of Indian unrest. When confinement to the reservation was enforced, the Paiute found that the resources on the reservation, which included fish, pine nuts, and roots, were not sufficient to feed everyone. Winters were difficult, and the tribe members often suffered from hunger.

As antelope shaman and chief of the Paiute, Old Winnemucca was a father figure responsible for satisfying the needs of his people. When food was scarce he had to think of new ways to obtain it. Sometimes the government came through with provisions, but more often they did not. The funds allotted to territorial governors and Indian agents quite often did not find their way to those for whom they were intended. Thus, in 1864 Old Winnemucca decided on a new plan. He would take traditional Paiute dances and ceremonies in full tribal dress, which he knew fascinated white audiences, and bring them into the theaters. The profits could then be used to feed his people. Although Old Winnemucca disliked having to "sell out" and use the sacred rites of his people for money, survival was more important.

The first performances in Virginia City, Nevada, proved to be very successful. The show was billed as a "Unique Attraction" featuring Chief Winnemucca of the Paiute, his two daughters, and eight warriors. Winnemucca opened with a speech, with Sarah as translator, telling the audience that the Paiute were friends of the white people; that they had been asked to join the Plains Indians in a war against the whites but had refused. Then the troupe acted out scenes of traditional and current Paiute life: the War Dance, the Capture of a Bannock Spy, the Grand Scalp Dance, the Coyote Dance, and others. The critics ridiculed the shows as amateur theatrics, but the audiences approved.

Encouraged by the show's success in Virginia City, Old Winnemucca took the show on the road. In the fall of 1864, the company performed at the Metropolitan Theatre in San Francisco. Here, Old Winnemucca, Sarah, and Elma were referred to as the Royal Family of the Paiute. Sarah became Princess Sarah, a title that was to stay with her whenever her name appeared in the white world. In addition, her poised and fluent speech, beauty, and refined delivery made her an instant celebrity. During these

Sarah Winnemucca is pictured here in a stage costume of her own design.
(Nevada Historical Society)

performances she seemed to have discovered her vocation, that of spokesperson for the Paiute and go-between for the Paiute and white worlds. Once again the shows were a great success. Yet the expense of feeding and housing the players detracted from the profits, and Old Winnemucca returned to Pyramid Lake with little more than he had had when he started. On the positive side, the show did help to bring Paiute life, and Indian life in general, to a wider audience, thereby winning the sympathy and understanding of influential people.

Shortly after returning to Pyramid Lake in early 1865, Old Winnemucca found he had more to worry about than food shortages. The Paiute had been accused of stealing cattle and of killing two white miners. The U.S. cavalry, led by Captain Almond Wells, rode into the Pyramid Lake reservation to find the perpetrators, or so Wells said. Wells's men proceeded to kill every Paiute in sight, mostly women and children. Old Winnemucca and his band returned from a hunting expedition to find that 30 or so of their people were dead. Among the dead were two of Old Winnemucca's wives. Full of despair and hopelessness, Old Winnemucca took his people to live in the mountains where there could be no further contact with the white world. Sarah's mother, Tuboitonie, died that winter in the mountains.

After Old Winnemucca's departure, only about 600 Paiute remained on the reservation at Pyramid Lake. Sarah was among those who stayed, though she was the only member of her family to do so. Her sister Elma married a white man and moved to a ranch in Montana—Sarah was now without her dearest friend and closest companion. But she was with her people, and that was her greatest concern. That winter at Pyramid Lake was filled with hardships. Food supplies were low and starvation was always imminent. And if it hadn't been for a delivery of calico cloth and blankets from Indian Bureau officials, many would have died from exposure to the cold.

When spring came, the group's troubles did not end. White farmers continued to graze their cattle on Paiute land, and a large timber reserve, also on Paiute land, was claimed by a lumber company. In addition, the white settlers who had been ordered off the land by Governor Nye were returning. The Paiute were powerless to do anything. Every attempt they had made to stand up for their rights had been followed by brutal retaliation. In *Life Among the Piutes*, Sarah tells of an incident from this time in which a Paiute man purchased gunpowder from a white officer. Later that day this same Paiute was shot and killed by that officer's assistant for possessing the gunpowder.

If it was the U.S. government's policy to keep Indians in constant fear to keep them under control, nowhere did the policy succeed so well as on the Pyramid Lake Reservation. Although a group of "friendly" soldiers led by a Captain Jerome came to protect the Paiute at Pyramid Lake from a white posse in the summer of 1868, the Paiute remained fearful. They felt that they could not trust anyone but themselves. However, Captain Jerome, it turned out, could be trusted. He had come in response to Sarah's appeal for help and protection. Jerome brought food and supplies that the Paiute desperately needed. He also hoped to locate Old Winnemucca and his band and bring them back to Pyramid Lake.

In Captain Jerome, as in Governor Nye, many Paiute felt that they had found an important ally. Jerome's plan was to reunite all of the separated bands of Paiute and secure for them a safe, protected home. This plan coincided with Sarah's own wish, and she was quick to offer her help. She was sent by Jerome to Fort McDermit in Oregon to work as an interpreter and to try to find Old Winnemucca. For her work, she would be paid $65 a month.

When she arrived at Fort McDermit, which was not as yet an official reservation, Winnemucca was amazed at how well other bands of Paiute were being treated. They were well-clothed, well-fed, and seemed to be very content. This was in sharp contrast to the life of the Paiute at Pyramid Lake. Later that summer, Old Winnemucca and his band were found by Sarah's brother Natchez and led back to Fort McDermit. It was clear from the appearance of these people that they had endured many hardships: most were naked and terribly thin, and those who did have clothes wore mere rags. Many others in their group had not survived the winter.

Seeing that the Paiute were well treated at Fort McDermit, Sarah began searching for other dispersed bands of Paiute in the hope of bringing them back to Fort McDermit as well. When she returned to Pyramid Lake, Sarah found that more than 100 Paiute had died from a measles epidemic. However, the new Indian agent for Nevada, Major Henry Douglass, had a plan to improve conditions at Pyramid Lake Reservation by assigning individual farms to the Paiute and then protecting this property from white settlers. Douglass, through Captain Jerome, asked Sarah for her opinion on the Paiute situation. Sarah responded by writing a very moving and, as it turned out, influential letter to Douglass—a letter that was later widely circulated in Washington, D.C. Portions of it were also printed in the magazine *Harper's Weekly* and in Helen Hunt Jackson's *A Century of Dishonor*.

In the letter Sarah asked that "the Indians have a guarantee that they can secure a permanent home on their own native soil, and that [their] white neighbors be kept from encroaching on [their] rights." If this were provided along with the necessary education, then, said Sarah, "I warrant that the savage (as he is called today) will be a thrifty and law abiding member of the community."

Douglass had many plans for improving the quality of the Paiute's lives. Among them was the creation of a school on the reservation, with Sarah as its headmistress. But this was not to be. In early 1870, Douglass was removed from his post and replaced by a Baptist missionary. In addition, the government planned to close the reservation at Fort McDermit, where Sarah was trying to start a school for Paiute children. Sarah protested this move in a letter to the commissioner of Indian affairs, but to no avail. The reservation was lost. Sarah, however, never lost the desire to see her people educated.

Having lost the chance to operate her own school, Sarah tried for success of a more personal kind. In early 1871 she ran off with Edward Bartlett to Salt Lake City and got married. But Bartlett turned out to be a poor choice for a husband—he squandered what little money Sarah managed to save during their brief stay in Salt Lake City, and when that was gone, he pawned her jewelry and

The Winnemucca family endured many hardships in an effort to secure adequate living conditions for their people. Left to right, Sarah, Old Winnemucca, Natchez, Captain Jack, and an unidentified boy. (Nevada Historical Society)

spent that money too. Within a year Sarah left Bartlett and returned to Fort McDermit. Poor choices for husbands were to be Sarah's curse. She never was able to find happiness in marriage. And her enemies in the government and in the press often used her failed marriages as proof that she had questionable morals.

The ensuing years were as strife-filled as Sarah's short-lived marriage to Bartlett. In 1872, a sharp division arose among the Paiute at the outbreak of the Modoc War—some Paiute joined the Modoc tribe in its fight against white settlers, while others refused to take up arms. Although, in fact, few Paiute actually joined up with the Modoc's leader, Captain Jack, the Paiute were still accused of supporting the war. One repercussion was the arrest of Sarah's brother Natchez, who had challenged the authority of the Indian agent at Pyramid Lake. The agent sent Natchez to Alcatraz prison off the coast of San Francisco, and despite Sarah's letter-writing campaign protesting her brother's wrongful imprisonment, Natchez remained at Alcatraz for two years.

While the Paiute at Pyramid Lake continued to eke out a bare existence, things were looking up for the Paiute living at the newly created Malheur reservation in Oregon. The Indian agent there, S. B. Parrish, had taught the Paiute the much-needed skills of carpentry, farming, blacksmithing, and other trades, and he had ordered and overseen the construction of a schoolhouse. Sarah and Old Winnemucca visited Malheur in 1874 with thoughts of relocating there, and both witnessed the fruit of the Paiute's hard work. Fields of corn spread far and wide. Watermelons, potatoes, and turnips grew in abundance. Their fellow Paiute were well-clothed and healthy. Old Winnemucca decided that this was where he should bring his followers.

Upon moving to Malheur, Sarah quickly impressed Parrish with her intelligence and her willingness to work hard to make the community succeed; Parrish in turned impressed Sarah as someone who was sincerely concerned with improving the living conditions of the Paiute. Parrish soon appointed Sarah to the post of teacher's assistant at the school. This was perhaps the happiest period of her life. Her people were moving toward self-reliance: they were learning trades and farming, and, most important, the children were getting an education. And she was finally doing what she most wanted to do—teach.

However, President Ulysses S. Grant was at this very time shifting responsibility for Indian affairs from the Department of the Interior to the War Department. Sadly, this change led to Parrish's dismissal at Malheur. In 1876 he was replaced by Major William Rinehart—a change that proved unfortunate for the Paiute. Rinehart believed that the reservation land belonged not to the Paiute but to the government. This meant that the Paiute were merely servants, and, rather than allowing the Paiute to keep the fruits of their labor, Rinehart declared that they would be paid in vouchers that they could use to purchase goods at the agent's own store. Rinehart also allowed white settlers to stake out land on the reservation. It was not long before the Paiute had had enough of Rinehart's policies. After all of their hard work, they now watched as their crops were sold off the reservation to the benefit of whites. Their plentiful supplies of food and goods were reduced to rations, and instead of living in prosperity, they now faced possible starvation.

Rinehart had also closed down the school, and since that time, Sarah had had nothing to do but fight Rinehart. For her it seemed as though it was Pyramid Lake all over again. She and a group of Paiute leaders went to Fort Harney to try to get Rinehart removed. Hearing of this, Rinehart quickly banished her from the reservation. With that, Paiute leaders decided that Sarah should go to Washington, D.C., to lodge a formal complaint against Rinehart. But a more urgent problem arose when a group of Paiute left Malheur to join with the Bannock Indians. The Bannock had been stirred by the recent uprising of the closely related Nez Percé, led by Chief Joseph, and had decided to take up arms against the whites. In 1878, this action led to the Bannock War and to what was perhaps Sarah's greatest act of heroism.

While many Paiute willingly joined the Bannock Indians in the war, others did not. Many of those Paiute who did not wish to fight were taken hostage by the Bannock, including Old Winnemucca and his band. One night, Sarah, working with the U.S. cavalry, sneaked into the Bannock camp at Lake Juniper in Oregon and led about 40 of the Paiute hostages out of the camp and into the hills, where the cavalry waited to escort them to safety. The cavalry captain was so struck by Sarah's act of bravery that he employed her as a scout for the remainder of the war. And word of Sarah's heroics made it into the papers. In San Francisco, where she was still remembered as "Princess Sarah," one paper wrote that she "had undergone hardships and dared dangers that few men would face."

After the Bannock War, the Paiute were left without a home. Most Paiute refused to return to Malheur and the abuses of Agent

Rinehart. For Old Winnemucca, it was time to return to his true home along the Humboldt River in Nevada. Sarah, whose second marriage, a whirlwind affair with Joseph Satwaller, had recently broken up, was sent to Washington, D.C., to see if he would be permitted to do so. In January 1880, she met with the secretary of the interior and with President Rutherford B. Hayes. She told them the history of the Paiute's struggles and about the abuses they had suffered under ruthless Indian agents. Her words were so compelling that she won over the secretary. Through his influence she was able to secure a promise that the land at Malheur would be granted to the Paiute to do with as they wished (Old Winnemucca's homeland at Pyramid Lake had been settled by whites and could not be returned to the Paiute).

During her visit to Washington, when she was not meeting with government officials Sarah spent her time speaking to other influential people. She hoped both to make money for her people and to win sympathy. She did not make much money, but she did take home promises of aid from some important friends, many of whom would later come through with helpful donations.

The success of the 1880 trip prompted Sarah to return to the East in 1883. She went to Boston, accompanied by her third husband, Lewis H. Hopkins. Finally, Sarah seemed to have selected a worthy spouse. Hopkins shared Sarah's concern for the Paiute and worked to arrange speaking engagements for her. He also served as her secretary. The trip to Boston turned out to be highly productive. Sarah met many important figures and made many friends, one of whom, Elizabeth Palmer Peabody, later donated money for Sarah to start a school on the Paiute reservation. Another friend, Mary Tyler Mann, widow of the famous educator Horace Mann, edited and in 1883 helped publish Sarah's book, *Life Among the Piutes, Their Wrongs and Claims*.

Of all the work Sarah did to promote the cause of her people, none of it had as great an effect as *Life Among the Piutes*. And in putting pen to paper, Sarah showed that she could write with as much eloquence and emotion as she displayed when speaking before an audience. With the book's publication, there came many invitations to speak, and the government took immediate steps to address the Paiute problems. Senator Henry Dawes, famous for his involvement with Indian issues, asked Sarah to his home to discuss the situation of her people. Dawes later used his influence to bring before Congress a bill that would declare the land around Fort McDermit a Paiute reservation. Unfortunately, Dawes's efforts were defeated.

Although Sarah knew this was the beginning of the end for her people, she returned with more than a gleam of hope. She had received money from Peabody to start a school, and she supplemented the funds with proceeds from the sale of her book. Her plan was to provide Paiute children with a basic education and fluency in English so that they, in turn, could become teachers. This way, education could spread rapidly thoughout Paiute culture. In 1885 she gathered a group of 25 Paiute children and began teaching them gospel songs in English. Her method of teaching was highly rhythmic and was based on her belief that if the children could speak the words phonetically (by sound) then their meaning would follow—an idea that has recently been praised as an "innovation" under the term *phonics.*

Although Winnemucca had no formal training in teaching, her methods were highly successful. Unlike most non-Indian educators at schools for Indians, Winnemucca did not try to replace Indian culture with white culture. As a Paiute, her foremost concern was the preservation of Paiute culture. Because of this emphasis, the Indian Bureau refused to acknowledge the school and help pay for the costs of running it, and this lack of support ultimately led to its demise.

The school, called the Peabody Indian School after its patron, operated from 1885 to 1889. But its final years were not as successful as its early ones. In 1887, the Dawes, or General Allotment, Act, sponsored by none other than Senator Henry Dawes, was passed in Congress. Among its many provisions for restructuring Indian landholding and culture was the requirement that all Indians be educated in non-Indian, English-speaking boarding schools, all of which would be located some distance from the students' reservations.

Sarah refused to give up her school, but her students were taken forcibly from her. Other students came, but the school's funding dropped off. To make things worse, Sarah's husband, who was suffering from tuberculosis, took money that had been put aside for the operation of the school and in 1889 went to San Francisco. He died before the year was out, and his end was followed soon after by the end of the Peabody School. Winnemucca had lost the two things that made life worth living for her: her husband and her school. To make matters worse, she too had contracted tuberculosis, and, in her weakening condition, had to seek a more hospitable climate. Though she was only 43 years old, life held little promise for her.

In 1889 Sarah went to live with her sister Elma at Henry's Lake, Idaho. The two sisters, who had taken such different paths in life, were united once again. Sarah had elected to fight for her culture, and because of that decision, she had endured a life of hardship and suffering. Yet it was not a life without some happiness and satisfaction. At last, perhaps wearied by years of struggle, Sarah decided to live in peace, away from the sorrows and suffering on the Paiute reservation. She never returned to her people. She died of tuberculosis on October 17, 1891, at Elma's cabin.

Sarah did not live to see the improvements that the 20th century brought to Paiute life—how her people moved toward self-sufficiency, and how they assimilated into the white world without giving up their traditional culture. But these improvements in the quality of Paiute life today owe a great deal to Sarah Winnemucca. Her writings brought the Paiute and their troubles into the public eye and exposed the corruption of Indian agents. Her school was a forerunner of modern schools that aim to preserve rather than destroy Indian culture, and her life served as a model for those who dream of a better life and who are determined to realize that dream.

SOARING ARROWS

◆ ◆ ◆

The La Flesche Family

In 1818 the last chief of the Omaha was born. His name was Joseph La Flesche, or "Iron Eyes." He was the son of a French fur trader whose name, La Flesche, means "arrow" or "shooting arrow," and an Indian woman. As a young man he was adopted into the Omaha tribe, whose homeland was located in the northeast corner of what is now Nebraska, by Chief Big Elk, who had taken a strong liking to the boy. Although Joseph, after succeeding Big Elk as chief of the Omaha, was to achieve fame in his own right, today he is known more as the father of three remarkable children than for anything he himself did. It is rare enough for one child in a family to achieve any kind of fame, but to have three children go on to win renown in three very different fields is incredible. And for three children growing up with all the social, economic, and educational disadvantages that crippled Native Americans in the 19th century, such a feat becomes even more amazing. Yet this is exactly what happened in the La Flesche family.

Although Joseph held a very traditional role as chief of the Omaha, he had converted to Christianity as a young man and was strongly in favor of the assimilation of the Omaha people into white culture. Joseph knew that non-Indians could not be defeated by force; there were just too many of them. He believed that the best way for his tribe to assimilate was for them to turn to farming as a livelihood. Setting himself up as an example, Joseph built a two-story house, with the bottom story serving as a trade store, and fenced in the surrounding land for farming. And in 1854, when Presbyterian missionaries started a school on the newly established Omaha reservation, Joseph recognized the opportunities that this school would provide for his children.

In addition to his personal activities, Joseph did his best to discourage traditional Omaha rituals; this later became a great source of friction between him and his son, Francis. But as chief of the Omaha, he understood the symbolic importance of his participation in the ancient Omaha ceremonies and events of the earthlodge, and he always took his children along. There was perhaps only one way in which Joseph was traditional, and that was with respect to marriage. In keeping with the Omaha customs, Joseph married more than once. His first wife was Mary Gale, the daughter of an Omaha woman and a white army surgeon.

Susette La Flesche

Omaha Activist and Public Speaker
(1854–1902)

◆ ◆ ◆

In the year 1854 Mary Gale gave birth to Joseph's first child, a daughter. She was given the name Inshtatheamba, or "Bright Eyes." From the beginning, Joseph taught his children the importance of learning to speak English. Too many problems, he knew, arose from the Indians' inability to communicate with white people. In addition to sending his own children to the mission schools, he insisted that other Omaha do the same, going so far as to hire a tribal "truant officer" to make sure that Omaha children attended the school. And he donated money to help build the school.

When "Bright Eyes" began school in 1861, a new name, Susette, went with her—a non-Indian name for her first entrance into the non-Indian world. In school, Susette exceeded even Joseph's high expectations. She soon became proficient in English and was asked to teach Reverend Burtt, the head missionary, how to speak Omaha. She also helped him compose sermons in the Omaha language. In exchange for this instruction, Burtt lent her books. Soon she was reading English as if it were her first language, becoming one of the most fluent speakers of English among the Omaha. Unfortunately, at the end of the Civil War in 1865, the Presbyterian mission was removed from the reservation, and the school was closed.

Within a year, however, Susette was back in school. A former teacher at the Presbyterian school named Nettie Read had begun teaching at a girls' school in Elizabeth, New Jersey, and through Reverend Burtt, arrangements were made for Susette to go east to this school. It was with great joy, and no small amount of trepidation, that Susette made her first venture into the "civilized" world of the eastern United States. At first, Susette was homesick and had problems adjusting to white customs, but she was equal to the challenge, and soon became a popular member of her class. Despite her limited education on the Omaha reservation, she succeeded in her studies just as well as, if not better than, most of her white classmates.

In 1875, at the age of 21, Susette graduated with honors from the Elizabeth Institute for Young Ladies. Her ambition was to return to her people and put her education to use in helping them, so upon her return home, Susette wrote to the Indian Bureau asking for a teaching position. She requested that, because there was a shortage of qualified teachers on the Omaha reservation and because she spoke the language, she be employed among her own people. The bureau replied that they were very impressed by Susette's background and would do their best to find her a position. Soon afterward Susette was offered a teaching job among the Pawnee. She eagerly accepted, but when she told Joseph of her plans, he insisted that she not go. He had heard of problems among the Pawnee—that many had died of disease and war in the past year—and he did not want his daughter going there.

Susette wrote and thanked the bureau, but asked again if she might teach among the Omaha. She also approached the Omaha agent, Colonel Furnas, directly. He told her that there was no need for more teachers. Susette countered by saying that there might not be a need for additional teachers, but there was certainly a need for *qualified* teachers. Furthermore, there were no Omaha teachers employed at the reservation's day school. Susette knew that, according to the laws of the reservation, Omaha who were qualified for jobs on the reservation had to be offered positions before any job was offered to an outsider. She read the law to Colonel Furnas, but he would not budge. She wrote to the administrators at the Indian Bureau, told them of her rejection by Furnas, and cited the reservation law. The bureau was slow to respond, but finally they wrote back offering her the job of assistant teacher at the Omaha agency school. She soon learned, however, that she would be paid only half the salary paid to white teachers.

Clearly, Susette was the victim of discrimination. But her grievance was a small one compared to the problems facing her people or, more specifically, their neighbors to the north, the Ponca. The Omaha and the Ponca were closely related. Their languages and customs were similar, they had a long tradition of friendship, and they had often fought side by side against their enemies. This time the Omaha and Ponca had a common enemy—the U.S. government. In 1877, the Ponca were ordered by the United States to leave their traditional hunting grounds along the Niobrara River, where their reservation was located, and move to Indian Territory, located in what is now Oklahoma and the regions bordering it. Standing Bear, chief of the Ponca, appealed to the Omaha for help. Joseph said that if the Ponca must move, they were always welcome on the Omaha reservation.

But the United States, fearing the unified power of the two tribes, forbade the Ponca to move onto the Omaha reservation. They must, said government officials, find a desirable tract of land in the new territory. Soldiers came to both the Ponca and Omaha reservations to enforce the removal. Reluctantly, the Ponca picked up and left the land of their ancestors. It would be useless to fight against the military strength of the U.S. army. The Ponca marched 500 miles to their new home, many dying on the way. Those who survived the journey discovered that the government had made no preparation

Susette La Flesche, the celebrated "Bright Eyes," was a tireless crusader for the Ponca cause and the rights of all Native Americans. (Nebraska State Historical Society)

for their arrival, as had been promised. Moreover, the land was hot and arid, and farming was difficult, if not impossible.

During these difficult times, Susette was greatly concerned for the plight of the Ponca. Gradually she was drawn in as a major figure in their struggle. Because of her fluency in English, she was asked to translate letters dictated to her by Chief Standing Bear— letters of protest that were sent to the U.S. Congress, the secretary of the interior, and the president. Susette also served as an interpreter between the Ponca and the U.S. representatives sent out to investigate the Ponca's claims. In addition, because of her knowledge of the injustices committed against the Ponca, and of the tragedies that befell them during their removal, Susette was asked to compose letters herself. But Susette's biggest contribution to the Ponca cause, the one that was to make her the most famous Indian woman since Pocahontas, was to come later.

Nearly a year after the Ponca removal to Indian Territory, Standing Bear decided that he could no longer watch his people starve. Supplies and farming provisions promised by the U.S. government had never been delivered. To make matters worse, malaria was spreading through the tribe and had already claimed the life of his son. As the boy's life waned, Standing Bear promised him that he would be buried with his sister on sacred land. In protest of the government's broken promises, and embittered by the forced removal of his people, Standing Bear and a group of more than 60 mourning Ponca loaded the boy's body onto a wagon and set out to return to their traditional homeland. Along the way, however, they were intercepted by soldiers, arrested, and put in jail.

The arrest of Standing Bear created a great stir in Nebraska. One man who became aware of the Ponca misfortunes through Standing Bear's imprisonment was Thomas Henry Tibbles, a journalist who had been active in the movement to free black slaves before the Civil War. Tibbles eagerly embraced the Ponca cause. He helped Standing Bear issue a formal request to Congress asking that the Ponca be allowed to return to their ancestral home. When this failed, he enlisted the help of A. J. Poppleton, a leading attorney of the day. Poppleton issued a writ of *habeas corpus*, a common law designed to protect people who are wrongfully imprisoned. The writ was a success, and the suit, *Ponca v. the United States,* went to trial. After much testimony, and a great deal of national attention, the Ponca won their case. Their removal was declared illegal by a court of law, and the Ponca were allowed to return to their tribal lands.

The Ponca had won a major victory. But, as Tibbles knew, the decision of the lower court could still be overturned by an act of Congress. Furthermore, other Indian tribes had been less fortunate in suing the government. Thus, he needed to increase awareness of the Ponca situation. He also wanted to extend his crusade to include all Indian tribes, and he hoped to win for Indians the right to be treated as equal subjects under the Constitution. At that time, Indians were considered wards of the United States; they did not have any rights and were not considered citizens. Tibbles decided to begin his crusade with a consciousness- and fund-raising tour of big cities. But he needed the help of two key people. One, of course, was Standing Bear. No one could speak for his people as well as their chief. The other key person whom Tibbles asked to help was a sur- prise—it was Susette La Flesche. After seeing copies of the letters Susette had written on behalf of the Ponca, Tibbles asked her to write a brief history of the Ponca troubles as she knew them. And when Tibbles decided to go east to raise money for the Ponca defense, he brought Susette along as an interpreter.

The trip could not have been more urgent. In early 1879, the Omaha learned that a bill had been introduced in Congress ordering their removal to Indian Territory. It seemed that the Omaha might have to undergo the same ordeal that the Ponca had just endured. Tibbles's group journeyed from St. Louis to Chicago, from Chicago to New York, and finally settled for awhile in Boston. At first, Susette was reluctant to join the group. She preferred to stay out of the spotlight and to help her people in small ways. But the big-city newspapers, drawn by Susette's stately demeanor and earnest speeches, made her a center of attention. Because of the newspaper publicity, the group was soon filling large halls. Their audiences grew and grew.

The La Flesche family first gained notoriety in 1879 when Francis and Susette, pictured here, joined Thomas Henry Tibbles and Standing Bear on a lecture tour in the northeastern United States. (Nebraska State Historical Society)

During her stay in Boston, Susette met many famous people—literary figures, politicians, theologians, and wealthy businessmen. In fact, Henry Wadsworth Longfellow presented her with a signed copy of his poem "Hiawatha," which was about a fictional Indian warrior. But the person who was to have the greatest influence on Susette was the writer Helen Hunt Jackson, who was just becoming interested in the Indian cause. Jackson's interest in the violation of Indian rights led to her famous condemnation of U.S. Indian policy, the book *A Century of Dishonor.*

It was because of Jackson's urging that Susette decided to take up the pen and tell the Indians' side of the story. In essays and short stories, Susette gave non-Indians a heretofore unavailable glimpse of what it meant to be an American Indian, of what Indian life was really like. Such an understanding, as Helen Hunt Jackson well knew, was the best way to dispel the image of the Indian as a ruthless savage, an image often used by the Indian Bureau to justify their mistreatment of Indians.

In her writings Susette fought back using her own powerful images of Indian suffering. In her story "Ploughed Under, The Story of an Indian Chief," she writes: "The huge plow of the Indian system has run for 100 years, beam down, turning down into the darkness of the earth every hope and aspiration which [Indians] have cherished. What sort of harvest will it yield to the nation whose hand has guided the plow?"

After a few months on the road, most of the people in Tibbles's group were tired and homesick. Only Tibbles had been back to Nebraska, after the death of his wife. Philadelphia was to be the last stop on their tour. By then Congress was holding hearings on the Ponca case, and Susette, along with Tibbles and Standing Bear, was asked to testify. In Washington, they met with Senator Dawes, an advocate of Indian rights, and helped him draw up a bill that would allow the Ponca to return to their old lands. (This bill was later pushed aside by Congress and was never ratified.) The hearings went well for the Ponca, despite strong opposition from the Indian Bureau, which claimed that the Ponca were happy in Indian Territory.

Susette anxiously awaited Congress's decision. Would all of the hard work of the past year pay off? Could the Ponca reclaim their land? Yes, they could! The Senate committee decided that the Ponca had been wrongfully removed from their land, and ruled that they could either return to their old land or remain in Indian Territory—the choice was theirs. In addition, the Ponca were to be paid $165,000 for the suffering caused by their removal; and farming equipment would be provided to them; and schools would be built.

But, as is often the case, problems developed in the execution of the decision. The Indian Bureau, which had fought Congress all along, was adamant about keeping the Ponca in Indian Territory. Apparently through coercion, and possibly through the use of liquor, the Indian Bureau produced a document, signed by all of the Ponca chiefs, proving that the Ponca wished to stay in Indian Territory. These signatures had been obtained before the chiefs received word that they could return to their old land. In the end, a compromise was reached. Although most of the Ponca who had been forced to move were not allowed to return to their original homeland, an agreement in May of 1881 set aside part of their homeland for those who had not claimed land in the new territory. Thus, Susette's hard work had not been in vain.

When the congressional hearings were over, Susette returned home and resumed teaching in the agency school. But something had happened while she was away—she and Tibbles had fallen in love. They were married in the spring of 1881. At first, the couple lived in Tibbles's house in Omaha, and he returned to his editorial work. Susette, no longer teaching, joined anthropologist Alice Fletcher in her efforts to gain citizenship for the Omaha, in the hope of readying them for the impending implementation of a new policy by the U.S. Congress. The policy, which was later incorporated into the Dawes Act and passed in 1887, required all Indians to choose parcels of land, or allotments, on their reservations, to which they would then be given individual title. After the parceling out was complete, their identities as members of particular tribes would be effectively lost. But before they could stake a claim to land, the Indians first had to be registered as U.S. citizens. Although they thought that they were becoming full citizens of the United States and would be granted all of the rights that went with this status, their citizenship was, in fact, conditional. The Indians had to prove that they were "competent," meaning that they must make good use of their land and that they must sever all ties to tribal organizations and societies. Sensing that it was in the Omaha's best interests to be in as much control as possible of the allotment process, Susette and Fletcher traveled around the agency, registering tribe members for citizenship and urging them to seek out fertile land.

In 1883, the allotment system was implemented officially on the Omaha reservation. Susette and Tibbles decided to move back to the reservation, and they selected an allotment in Logan Valley, a fertile area where Joseph had also chosen to live. Tibbles tried his hand at farming, but it was clearly not his forté. Their first year's corn harvest was small, and the market price for corn was low.

Susette, in the meantime, saw a chance to supplement the little money that came from farming and from Tibbles's writing. She served as technical advisor on Helen Hunt Jackson's novel *Ramona* published in 1884. The book tells the tragic story of the Indians' struggles against white invaders and the abuses of government agents. Although the book was not a critical success, it offered the non-Indian reader a rare insight into Indian life and became one of the most popular books of the period.

The novel came to the attention of Major Pond, a New York lecture agent, who suggested that Susette and Tibbles go on a speaking tour of England. After years of being out of the public spotlight, Susette agreed to do the tour. In 1887, the couple once again hit the lecture circuit, speaking before large audiences, primarily in and around London. After one speaking engagement, they were introduced to British Prime Minister William Gladstone, who questioned Susette at great length about the Indian situation. From London, the couple went to the Midlands of England, and then on to Scotland. They spent nearly a full year in England, returning home in 1888. When they arrived back in Logan Valley, they found that Joseph had become ill.

He was not to recover. Susette took her father's death badly and vowed never to leave home again.

Tibbles, on the other hand, could not sit still. He was happiest when he had a cause to pursue, and in 1893, populism became that cause. The populist movement, which began in the 1890s, sought to protect the rights of and support the views of the "common man." The Populist party's main objective was to represent the individual farmer against the abuses of farm monopolies. Tibbles was not much of a farmer, but the difficulties he had experienced enabled him to sympathize with other struggling farmers. His involvement with the populist movement required a great deal of travel, and he convinced Susette to move to Washington, D.C. for a year while he worked for the *The Nonconformist*, a populist newspaper. In 1902, after the populist cause had lost much of its following, Tibbles even became the party's candidate for vice president.

But Susette was not eager to continue public life, preferring instead to live near her family and among the Omaha. She now had five children of her own to raise and wanted them to be immersed in Omaha culture. Susette saw that the best service she could do for her people was to lead by example. It was important that the La Flesches, descendants of the last chief of the Omaha, succeed as farmers. Many Omaha who had received land through the Dawes Act either sold or were cheated out of their land by white men. Of course, when the money from the sale ran out (often it was squandered on alcohol, which was readily proferred by whites), they had no means of livelihood. Susette never forgot her father's advice: Indians must learn the ways of white people if they are to survive. She spent the remainder of her life trying to realize her goal of proving to non-Indians that Indians were as capable and intelligent as whites, and therefore deserved the same rights.

Susette died in late 1902 after a brief illness. Hearing of her worsening condition, Tibbles had rushed home from Omaha, Nebraska, arriving just hours before her death. On her grave, he carved the epitaph: "She did all she could to make the world happier and better."

Francis La Flesche

Omaha Ethnologist
(1857–1932)

◆ ◆ ◆

Francis La Flesche, the third of Joseph's children (the first with Elizabeth Esau), was born in 1857. Like his half-sister Susette before him, Francis distinguished himself at the Presbyterian mission school. And also like Susette, Francis took an active interest in Omaha culture. As a boy, he served as the "Sacred Child" in the Wawan or pipe ceremony, and he went through the traditional Omaha rites of manhood. Francis also participated in the last Omaha buffalo hunt while he was still in his teens. He was a strong and willful young boy, and he often got into arguments with his father. Although both men revered Omaha custom, Joseph believed that the past should take a back seat to progress and assimilation. Francis, on the other hand, grew to value Omaha culture above all else.

When Susette embarked on her momentous speaking tour with Standing Bear and Thomas Tibbles in 1879–80, Francis was asked to go along. This visit was to change the direction of the young man's life. In Washington, on the last leg of their tour, he met anthropologists Alice Fletcher and George Dorsey who specialized in the study of Indian culture. Dorsey later gave Francis valuable training in linguistics, but it was Fletcher who was to become a major influence and companion for the remainder of his life. When Fletcher's work brought her to the Omaha reservation a year later, she asked Francis to serve as her field assistant and interpreter. So pleased was she with Francis's research abilities and hard work that she soon came to think of him as a partner; she gave him credit as coauthor in various articles and in her book *The Omaha Tribe* (1911).

The initial meeting with Fletcher had taught Francis sound research methods, and he soon began to apply these methods to interests of his own. A look at Francis's long list of publications shows just how tireless a worker he was. His first article, "The Sacred Pipes of Friendship," was published in 1885 by the

American Association for the Advancement of Science. He also began his studies of the Osage Indians at about this time. The Osage and his own Omaha people had a history of close ties—ties that came about from living near one another and, because the two tribes' languages were similar, from constant communication. He also wrote a book of personal memories of his education at the Presbyterian mission school, which was later incorporated into his book, *The Middle Five* (1901).

The Middle Five, the title of which refers to the tribes that spoke the dialect of Dhegiha—the Omaha, the Kansa, the Quapaw, the Osage, and the Ponca—investigates the life and education of Indian boys on the reservations of the Dhegiha Sioux, which included Francis's own Omaha tribe as well as the Osage, Kansa, Ponca, and Quapaw. In this work, Francis gave much credit to the quality of education provided to Indians by Presbyterian missionaries, using his own eloquence and intelligence as a testament to the quality of this education. It was also Francis's aim to dispel the image of Indian boys as wild, uncultivated savages—an image then popular among purveyors of Wild West shows and boys' adventure stories.

As if his ethnological work were not enough to keep him busy, Francis also tried his hand at writing opera. He collaborated with composer Charles Cadman on a three-act piece called *Da-Oma, The Land of Misty Waters*. Unfortunately, there is no record of the opera's ever having been performed, and it was never published. It appears that after this failure, Francis realized where his talents lay and never ventured into the arts again.

In the 1890s Francis decided to complete his formal education by registering for classes at the University of Nebraska. Despite all of the projects he was juggling at the time, Francis completed a bachelor's degree in language and literature in 1892, and then a master's degree in 1893. The University of Nebraska later honored his life and work by presenting him with a doctorate degree.

This education was of enormous help to Francis, for he began to write with great ease and skill, and his production of articles and books continued at a steady pace. Following his graduation, Francis moved to Washington, D.C., to be with Fletcher, and their

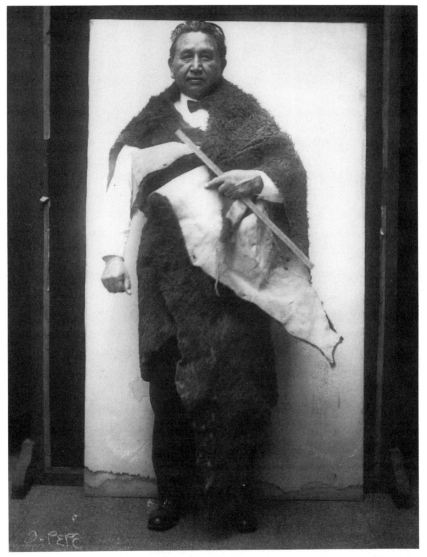

When Francis La Flesche was hired by the Smithsonian Institution in 1911, he became the first Native American professional ethnographer. He is pictured here draped in a buffalo hide. (Smithsonian Institution)

collaboration resumed. He and Fletcher immediately set to work completing and organizing the research that they had done on the Omaha during the preceding 10 years. During this time Francis also finished *The Middle Five* and published a series of articles,

including important studies of Omaha Buffalo Medicine Men—
the priestlike holy men and healers who figured so prominently
in many Indian cultures.

Information from these and other articles was included in what
is arguably his and Fletcher's greatest achievement, *The Omaha
Tribe*, which appeared in 1911. This massive, 700-page book provided a revealing look at the history and culture of a people such
as had never been written before. The book was to become a classic
study in ethnology (the study of cultures), an accomplishment
that would serve as a model for future Indian studies.

With the publication of *The Omaha Tribe*, Francis became widely
recognized as a leading Native American ethnologist. One important source of recognition came from the Smithsonian Institution
in Washington. In 1911, shortly after his book came out, the
Smithsonian commissioned Francis to study and prepare annual
reports on the Osage tribe. Francis gratefully accepted the position, thus becoming the first Native American professional anthropologist. For the next 18 years, Francis collected and recorded
an enormous amount of information on the Osage and faithfully
published it in his annual reports.

While studying the Osage, Francis learned that many of the
tribe's traditional ceremonies and rituals were disappearing at an
alarming rate. Realizing that these ceremonies had to be observed
and recorded immediately or be lost forever, Francis focused on
this area. In all, he compiled more than 2,000 pages of data on the
Osage, including translations of creation myths, songs, and
chants. For example, Francis recorded the ancient Osage "Child-
Naming Rite," which features a chant that invokes supernatural
powers to guarantee a long, peaceful life and a continuous line of
descendants. A sample from the chant attests to the beauty and
poetry that are a part of the Osage Rite:

> There comes a time
> When a calm and peaceful day comes upon me
> So shall there come upon the little
> ones a calm and peaceful day,
> As they travel the path of life.

Considering that many Osage feared supernatural punishment for revealing tribal secrets to an outsider, the amount of material that Francis was able to collect is astonishing. And although Francis was never able to organize all of this research in book form, it was a valuable source for later work on the Osage, such as in John Joseph Mathews's *The Osage.*

In 1927, Francis, now almost 70 years old, continued to work at the tireless pace of a young man. Four years earlier he had lost his colleague, best friend, and closest companion, Alice Fletcher. It seems as though Francis's way to cope with this personal tragedy was to bury himself in his work, which is probably what Fletcher would have wanted him to do. However, while hurrying to complete his work on an Osage dictionary, he had a physical breakdown, from which he never fully recovered. And with this illness, his distinguished scholarly career came to an end. After the breakdown, he moved back to the Omaha reservation and lived out the remaining five years of his life. He died in his brother's home in 1932.

Susan La Flesche

Omaha Physician
(1865–1915)
◆ ◆ ◆

The youngest of the celebrated La Flesche children was Susan. Born in 1865, Susan was much younger than Susette and Francis. She was, therefore, still a child when her elder siblings were making a name for themselves. But she benefited greatly from seeing by their success that opportunities were open for Native Americans. Joseph also instilled in her the ambition to succeed in the competitive world outside the reservation.

Because she was a La Flesche, a great deal was expected of her at the mission school. And she did not disappoint. But by the time Susan was ready for school in 1870, education and civilization on the Omaha reservation had changed as a result of the "Quaker Policy" of 1869, which gave Quaker missionaries control of the reservation's schools. Still, the quality of education seems to have been as good as, if not better than, that provided by the Presbyterian missionaries. And like the Presbyterians before them, the Quakers believed in educating both boys and girls. However, a large part of the girls' education consisted of domestic training, which meant learning to cook, sew, and do laundry. In addition, the Quakers introduced a new dimension in this domestic training, something in which Susan took a special interest—caring for the sick.

When Susan completed her training at the Quaker mission school in 1879, Joseph sent her and her sister Marguerite to the Elizabeth Institute for Young Ladies in New Jersey, the same school Susette had attended a few years earlier. Here, Susan had her first real interaction with the white world. Although little is known about the two years she spent at Elizabeth, it appears that she got along well with her fellow students. Susan also must have performed well in her studies because, when she returned to the Omaha reservation in 1881, she was given a position as a teacher at the Quaker school.

Although Susan taught at the Quaker school for only two years, her return to the reservation was significant. By returning to the Omaha people, Susan discovered her vocation, for it was at this time that she decided to pursue her childhood ambition of becoming a medical doctor. Such a decision may not seem unusual to people today, but at that time there were very few women physicians, and there certainly were no female *Indian* doctors.

The first step Susan took toward realizing this dream was to enroll at the Hampton Institute in Virginia. (Established just after the end of the Civil War in 1868, the Hampton Institute was designed to give agricultural training to African-American freedmen. Native Americans began to be admitted to the school about 10 years later.) At Hampton, Susan was able to receive more academic training, but domestic skills still took up a large part of the curriculum. Susan excelled at Hampton and was salutatorian of her class in 1886.

Her academic success at Hampton brought her to the attention of many important people, among them Sara Thomson Kinney, president of the Connecticut Indian Association, and Dr. Martha Waldron, the school physician at Hampton. The latter's influence on Susan must have been particularly strong. Dr. Waldron urged Susan to inquire into the possibility of entering the Woman's Medical College of Pennsylvania, Waldron's own alma mater. Susan applied to the college and was accepted, but her request for a scholarship was denied. She was left with no way to pay her tuition. But her brother Francis and the famous Indian anthropologist Alice Fletcher were soon hard at work getting her financial support. When they contacted Sara Thomson Kinney and the Connecticut Indian Association, the funding problem was solved. An elated Susan wrote to Kinney to thank her for the assistance, saying that "it has always been a desire of mine to study medicine ever since I was a small girl, for even then I saw the needs of my people for a good physician."

The following fall, in 1886, Susan stepped off a train in Philadelphia and moved into a room at the YWCA. Although she had experienced life in a big, eastern city while at Elizabeth, this time she was alone. But she soon threw herself body and soul into her medical training. She studied chemistry, anatomy, physiology, and obstetrics. In a letter home, Susan joked that she was now using the scalpel knife, "not the scalping knife." Indeed, in her anatomy class, she spent a good deal of her time dissecting cadavers. Apparently, Susan did not have a weak stomach, and she was fascinated by her studies of the human body.

It wasn't long before Susan got a chance to apply her medical training. After she completed her first year at the college, she returned home to care for the victims of a measles epidemic at the Omaha reservation. She was also able to give her people some practical knowledge in preventive medicine, teaching them good everyday sanitary habits that would prevent the spread of disease. The value to the Omaha of this training program cannot be overestimated. Life-threatening diseases had been laying waste to Indian lives ever since the coming of the Europeans. These white settlers introduced diseases, such as smallpox and measles, for which the Indians had little or no

In 1889, Susan, seen here in this never-before-published photo (third row, fourth from left), graduated from the Women's Medical College of Pennsylvania at the top of her class, thus becoming the first Native American woman physician. (Medical College of Pennsylvania)

natural resistance. And inoculations against these diseases were not given to Indians for another 10 years. Consequently, epidemics often wiped out families, communities, and in some cases, entire tribes.

In March 1889, Susan completed her medical training. It was a monumental achievement. Not only was she the first American Indian woman to become a physician; she had done it in grand style by finishing as the top student in her class. After graduation, Susan served as resident assistant at the Woman's Hospital of Philadelphia. This position, however, was to occupy her only until she could convince the commissioner of Indian affairs to make her agency physician for the Omaha. Impressed by Susan's educational background and her past achievements, the commissioner created the position of Omaha agency physician, and placed Susan in charge of the health care of more than 1,200 Indians. Later on, she would take charge of the medical care of many white settlers in the region as well.

Susan's first real challenge as a doctor came in the winter of

1891, when an influenza epidemic struck the Omaha reservation. She drove herself in a horse and buggy across the reservation to visit her patients at home, sometimes driving miles in subzero temperatures. In that winter alone, she treated more than 600 patients. The job would have been too much for most people, and eventually the exhaustion of her work caught up with Susan. In 1893 she became ill and, because she was confined to her bed, had to resign her position. It is likely that Susan suffered from osteomyelitis, an infection of the bone that can cause deafness. This disease is rare today and is easily cured with antibiotics.

In late 1894, Susan began to regain her strength, but certain aspects of her illness remained, such as ear infections and headaches. It was also at about this time that Susan fell in love with and married Henry Picotte, a Sioux Indian and the brother of the man Susan's sister Marguerite had married. Susan and Henry settled in Bancroft, Nebraska, where Susan once again began to practice medicine. She helped to establish a medical center in her adopted town and for three years served as chairperson of the State Health Committee of the Nebraska Federation of Women. During this period, Susan fought such bad health habits as shared drinking cups and alcoholism, which had long been a problem among the Indians, and helped to get a hospital built.

Susan soon began to realize that the biggest health problem among her people was the consumption of alcohol. For one thing, American Indians were especially susceptible to cirrhosis of the liver (a hardening of the tissue often caused by excessive drinking), which still exists today as a major cause of death among American Indians. But as Susan saw it, cirrhosis of the liver was not the only danger of alcohol; it was the accidental deaths that often resulted from public drunkenness that worried her the most. In 1905, after years of excessive drinking, Susan's husband died from cirrhosis of the liver. This personal tragedy stirred Susan to action. Within two years of her husband's death, Susan began pressuring the Omaha Agency commissioner to ban the traffic of liquor on the reservation. But there was a great deal of money to be made in the sale of liquor to the Indians, and with money came power. As a result of pressure from liquor merchants, Susan never succeeded in ridding her people of one of their greatest foes. She had to be content with continuing to warn her patients about the dangers of excessive drinking.

It was perhaps this battle that led Susan to take up political as well as medical causes. A big issue on the Omaha reservation (and on many other Indian reservations) in the early 1900s was the reimbursement to Indians of money paid to the U.S. government for Indian land. According to the Dawes Act, after a certain period of time, all Indians with allotted lands were free to farm or sell the land as they pleased. Tribal lands that were "left over" after allotment were sold by the government to white settlers, with the understanding that the money from these sales would be divided equally among the Indians. However, payment was often slow in coming. In addition, many Indians were missed by census-takers, so their names did not appear on the list of Indians to receive payment. In most cases, these Indians were out of luck.

In 1910 the Omaha were fighting for the return of money that was rightfully theirs. Because of her education and because of the respect that her people had for her, Susan was named a delegate to argue on behalf of the Omaha before the secretary of the interior. Susan's first venture into Indian politics proved a success. The Omaha won their case before Congress. A new census was taken so that all Omaha could receive their share of the money.

Susan had gone to Washington at the urging of her people, but she knew that she was not fit for such travel. Although she was only in her mid-forties, she had never completely recovered from her illness of 1893. She was now nearly deaf from continuous ear infections. She decided to spend her time continuing to promote cleanliness and sanitary habits among her people. She battled against tuberculosis, a contagious disease that spread rapidly among the Omaha because of their tradition of sharing the same drinking cup. She also taught the Indians to rid their homes of insects and other carriers of disease through the use of window screens and disinfectants.

But these and other battles were not to be won in Susan's lifetime. On September 18, 1915, Susan died. The Omaha had lost their doctor, someone who had cared for them as they sometimes did not care for themselves. And her passing gave them a chance to reflect on her accomplishments. A local newspaper wrote, "Hardly an Omaha is living that has not been treated and helped by her, and hundreds of white people and Indians owe their lives to her care and nursing."

◆ ◆ ◆

Susette, Francis, and Susan La Flesche stand out as examples of what education and opportunity could and can do for Native Americans. But, beyond this, they represent the sort of people who, through education and intellectual ability, were able to assimilate into the white world, but who never forgot where they came from. The La Flesches used their education and intelligence to help better their own people. For all their achievements, it was this kind of devotion and allegiance to their people that was, perhaps, their most remarkable characteristic.

CHARLES A. EASTMAN (OHIYESA)

◆ ◆ ◆

Santee Sioux Physician and Writer
(1858–1939)

In *From the Deep Woods to Civilization,* Charles Eastman recalled the words that his father used to persuade him to go to the mission school in Flandreau, South Dakota:

> Here is one Sioux who will sacrifice everything to win the wisdom of the white man! We have now entered upon this life, and there is no going back. Besides, one would be like a hobbled pony without learning to live like those among whom we must live.

Young Ohiyesa was reluctant to go, and his first day at the school was indeed a disaster. The other students—American Indians like himself—made fun of him: unlike his classmates, his hair was long, in the traditional manner of the Sioux, and he spoke not a word of English. But he did not let the taunting stop him—"My father's logic was too strong, and the next day I had my long hair cut, and started to school in earnest." And he kept going to school, for the next 17 years in fact, until he finished medical school at the age of 32. In the course of his education he had gone from the deep woods of Manitoba, Canada, to class orator at Boston University

Medical School's graduation ceremony; from hunter and warrior to physician and intellectual. He would never be a "hobbled pony" in the white man's world.

Although Eastman painted a rather idealized picture of his childhood in his book *Indian Boyhood*, it truly was a difficult period for a boy growing up Sioux. Life for Eastman began with tragedy. His mother, Mary Nancy Eastman, died giving birth to him in February 1858 somewhere in what is now Minnesota. Because of this misfortune, the child was given the name "Hakadah," which means "the pitiful last" in Sioux.

His father, Many Lightnings, was a full-blooded Sioux and took part in the Sioux Uprising of 1862, in which hundreds of non-Indians were murdered. In retaliation, Many Lightnings, along with more than 300 other Santee Sioux, was sentenced to be hanged by the U.S. Army. Although no single cause for this uprising has been identified, it is certain that the Santee Sioux felt that they had been cheated out of land and money by white settlers and government officials in Minnesota. Thirty-eight of the Sioux held were actually hanged, and Many Lightnings's family presumed that he was among them, although they later learned otherwise.

While Many Lightnings was under arrest, Hakadah lived with his grandmother, Uncheedah. It was through her that Hakadah learned the traditional ways of his tribe. He listened carefully to his grandmother's stories and remembered them well enough as an adult to retell them in his books. He also learned about the Sioux religion, and about the god Wakan Tanka, or the Great Mystery. In his book *The Soul of the Indian*, Eastman describes the highest expression of the Sioux religion—*hambeday*, or "mysterious feeling":

> The first *hambeday* marked an epoch in the life of the youth, which may be compared to that of confirmation or conversion in Christian experience. Having first prepared himself by means of the purifying vapor-bath, and cast off as far as possible all human or fleshly influences, the young man sought out the noblest height in all the surrounding region. At the solemn hour of the sunrise or sunset he took up his position, overlooking the glories of the earth and facing the "Great Mystery," and there he remained, naked, erect, silent,

and motionless, exposed to the elements and forces of His arming for a night and a day. . . . Sometimes he would chant a hymn or offer the ceremonial pipe. In this holy trance or ecstasy the Indian mystic found his highest happiness and the motive power of his existence.

Eastman later converted to Christianity, but he liked to point out the similarities between his adopted religion and the Sioux religion, and he always respected and defended the faith of his ancestors against missionaries who insisted that the Sioux adopt Christianity.

It was during these early years that Hakadah received a new, more distinguished name. The Sioux placed a great value on the bravery of their young warriors, and they had devised a number of games to test a boy's bravery. One such game was lacrosse, a game that had originated with the Mohawk and spread to many other Indian tribes. The game was played much as it is today, using webbed sticks to hurl a ball through a goal. After leading his team to victory, Hakadah was renamed "Ohiyesa," or winner. In another test of bravery and initiation into manhood, Ohiyesa had to sacrifice to Wakan Tanka his most valued possession, his dog, so that the Great Mystery would make him a great hunter and warrior. During his training, he was taught by his uncle, Mysterious Medicine, that no white man from the United States was to be spared and that at no other time in the Sioux's history was it so necessary to have great warriors. White settlers and government agents continued to push the Sioux westward, and it appeared that they would have to fight to keep their land.

Most Santee Sioux, including Ohiyesa's family, fled Minnesota after the 1862 uprising. Ohiyesa was taken by his uncle to live on a farm in Manitoba, Canada. There he became a skilled hunter and lived the traditional life of a Sioux boy. There were no missionary schools where he lived, so he did not not learn English or any of the other skills that many Sioux children were learning in other areas. He was, however, taught the skills of the Sioux warrior, so that he would always be prepared to go to war, to defend his people, and to avenge his father's death. However, a miraculous thing happened in 1873 when Ohiyesa was 15 years old—his father showed up at his uncle's farm in Manitoba. Many Lightnings had not been one of those hanged during the Sioux Uprising but had had his sentence commuted, and had spent three years in a federal prison. All of a sudden Ohiyesa had a father again. But his father was no longer Many Lightnings; he was now Jacob Eastman and had converted to Christianity. Eastman describes the return of his father as the turning point in his life:

> One can never be sure of what a day may bring to pass. At the age of fifteen years, the deepening current of my life swung upon such a pivotal day, and in the course was utterly changed; as if a little mountain brook should pause and turn upon itself to gather strength for the long journey toward an unknown ocean.

For the time being, the brook swung toward the Sioux community of Flandreau, South Dakota, and the beginning of Ohiyesa's adjustment to the "civilized" life of the white world. This meant changing his name to Charles Alexander Eastman, living the life of a Christian, and speaking English. And Eastman adapted himself to this new life remarkably well. In his first two years at Santee Normal School, he learned English and math and studied the Bible. His scholarly abilities caught the attention of Joseph Riggs, the Presbyterian missionary who ran the school, and through Riggs Eastman won a scholarship to Beloit Preparatory College in Beloit, Wisconsin. Sadly, just before Eastman departed for Beloit, his father died—the great guiding influence of his life had once again been taken from him. His older brother John, with whom he had been reunited in Flandreau, insisted that Eastman continue his studies—Jacob would have wanted it that way.

Perhaps spurred on by the memory of his father, Eastman never looked back. From Beloit, he moved on to Knox College in Galesburg, Illinois, assisted again in gaining admission by Riggs, who was himself an alumnus of Knox. After two years at Knox, Eastman had proved himself able to compete intellectually in the non-Indian world, but he still did not know what profession he wanted to direct his studies toward. He wanted to choose a way of making a living that would also be of use to his people. "Gradually my choice narrowed down to law and medicine," stated Eastman in *From the Deep Woods to Civilization*. "The latter seemed to me to offer a better opportunity of service to my race." After consulting with Riggs, he made his decision: he would enroll at Dartmouth College, a former Indian school located in Hanover, New Hampshire. The transition from the backwoods of

Eastman (top left), pictured here with fellow athletes of the Dartmouth College class of 1887, set the school record for long-distance running and was captain of the football team. (Dartmouth College Special Collections)

Sioux country to the civilized world of the Ivy League was now complete.

But there was still the matter of hitting the books. In order to enter Dartmouth, Eastman had to spend a year and a half correcting certain shortcomings in his education. After those problems were solved, Eastman entered Dartmouth in 1883—a 25-year-old freshman who 10 years earlier had not been able to read, write, or speak English. In his preparations for medical school, Eastman took the Latin Scientific program of study, which required that he take courses in Latin, French, Greek, German, zoology, botany, philosophy, chemistry, physics, natural history, and political science, to name a few. Despite this heavy course load, Eastman still found time for sports. In this area, he lived up to his name Ohiyesa (winner): he was captain of the football team, played baseball and tennis, boxed, and set the school record for long-distance running.

During his summers off, Eastman remained in the East, often staying with Frank Wood, a prominent Indian reformer who lived in Boston. As an active lobbyist for Indian interests, Wood worked for Indian rights, advancement, and citizenship, and was instrumental in making Eastman an example of how beneficial education could be for American Indians. Wood arranged for Eastman to give talks before Indian sympathizers in the East, for which Eastman received handsome payments that helped ease the financial strains of student life. Whether giving or listening to lectures, Eastman got a more positive impression of the "civilized" white world that somewhat balanced what he had seen in the West. In the East, he met and conversed with such great literary figures as Matthew Arnold, Ralph Waldo Emerson, and Henry Wadsworth Longfellow. Contact with these men may have had much to do with Eastman's own literary ambitions later in life.

When Eastman graduated from Dartmouth in 1887, Wood helped him to obtain the financial support he needed to attend Boston University Medical School. Although Eastman had planned to return to Sioux country as a medical missionary after finishing at Dartmouth, Wood and other "friends of the Indian" had persuaded him to go on to medical school. However, the help of these generous people put a great deal of pressure on Eastman. It began to seem to him as though the whole issue of the Indian rights movement depended on his success. "A high ideal of duty was placed before me," said Eastman, "and I was doubly armed in my original purpose to make my education of service to my race." And he did not let his benefactors down. In June, 1890, he became Dr. Eastman, and was elected by his class to deliver the graduation speech.

Soon after graduation, Eastman headed out west. It must have been very strange for him to return to Sioux country—with the exception of one summer spent working in his brother's store, Eastman had been away for eight years. Nevertheless, he was determined to fulfill his original ambition. He applied to the commissioner of Indian affairs for the position of agency physician, preferably in Sioux country, where he felt his knowledge of the language and customs would make his job a good deal easier. He was finally offered the job of agency physician at Pine Ridge, a Sioux reservation located in the southwest corner of South Dakota. Eastman must have been pleased to be granted the position he wanted, but his life in the East had not prepared him for what awaited him on the Pine Ridge reservation. Ethnologist James Mooney described the reservation as the largest, wildest, and most militaristic of all the Sioux agencies. Upon his arrival, the new doctor was utterly swamped with patients, many of whom came merely out of curiosity, to see the "Indian white doctor." Although Eastman thought he was prepared for a new life of "roughing it," he was shocked nevertheless by what he found at Pine Ridge. Patients came to him with their own diagnoses of their sicknesses and expected to be given drugs instead of first being examined by the doctor.

If Eastman did not expect the lawlessness of life on the reservation, he also certainly did not expect that he would marry. In 1890, Elaine Goodale, an educator of Indians from Massachusetts, was named supervisor of education for the two Dakotas. Later that year she visited the Pine Ridge agency and met Eastman. Although the two had never met, they were far from strangers. Eastman had read some of Goodale's articles on Indian education, and Goodale had heard of the promising Sioux doctor from friends in the East. Eastman was deeply impressed by Goodale, and by her concern for Indian people. As Eastman later recalled, he had planned to devote himself to the medical care of his people, but he "had not given due weight to the possibility of love." It must have been love at first sight, for they were married in the early part of 1891.

By this time Eastman had settled into the life of a reservation doctor, which meant winning the trust of his patients and proving the value of non-Indian medicine and medical procedures. Although Eastman was an excellent and well-trained physician, many Sioux still sought the traditional cures of their medicine men. But this was a minor obstacle compared to what Eastman faced on December 31, 1890.

Since his coming to Pine Ridge, a new religion, called the Ghost Dance, which had been introduced to the Sioux two years earlier, had recently become more fervidly practiced at Pine Ridge. Followers of the Ghost Dance religion, founded by a Northern Paiute holy man named Wovoka, believed that the Great Spirit intended to swallow the white men up into the earth and restore the buffalo to the plains. By practicing the religion, believers were promised a return to their past glory and prosperity. The religion centered around the ritual Ghost Dance, which involved a slow side-stepping movement in a circle, trancelike visions, and meditation.

Despite the religion's emphasis on peace and nonviolence, many white officials viewed it as an excuse for Indians to get together and plan an uprising. They therefore feared its spread. In November of 1890, they banned the Ghost Dance on Sioux reservations. The white authorities' fear of the Ghost Dance became all too apparent at the dawn of 1891. Disaster struck when the U.S. Seventh Cavalry was sent to stop the movement of a band of Miniconjou Sioux, led by a chief named Big Foot, toward the Pine Ridge reservation. The officials feared that Big Foot and his people were planning to join the movement, but in fact, Big Foot had no such plans. He hoped to join up with other Sioux chiefs on the reservation who wanted to seek peace with the U.S. government.

The cavalry, numbering about 500, met up with Big Foot and his band of 350, about 230 of whom were women and children, at a place called Wounded Knee, and ordered the group to surrender its weapons and make camp. Most of the Indians complied, but a few refused, roused by the urgings of a medicine man named Yellow Bird. He told the Miniconjou warriors that bullets could not kill them because they were wearing their special Ghost Dance shirts. When soliders tried to disarm a deaf Indian named Black Coyote his rifle went off, and the shooting began. Most of the Miniconjou had been disarmed when the fighting broke out and were defenseless. The conflict ended in a brutal massacre that left about 150 Indians dead and 44 injured. In the killing, soldiers did not discriminate between warriors and women and children.

Earlier that day, Eastman had watched the Seventh Cavalry depart from Pine Ridge toward Wounded Knee. He knew that there would be trouble. In fact, he protested the summoning of troops by his supervisor, Daniel Royer. Soon after the fighting began, members of the cavalry rode in carrying wounded Indians. Eastman spent most of the night attending to the wounded in the mission chapel. The next day, Eastman and his wife organized a rescue party and made the 18-mile trip, by horse and through a driving blizzard, to Wounded Knee. When they reached the scene of the massacre, the sight was almost too much for him and his party to bear. As Eastman wrote later:

> It took all of my nerve to keep my composure in the face of this spectacle, and of the excitement and grief of my Indian companions, nearly every one of whom was crying aloud or singing his death song.

Eastman and his party searched the piles of bodies covered in snow. To his amazement, he did find survivors. Among the living whom he found, he was most struck by an old blind woman huddled under a wagon, and by a warmly wrapped baby lying amidst the dead bodies. In *From the Deep Woods to Civilization*, Eastman recalled his feeling that "all this was a severe ordeal for one who had so lately put all his faith in the Christian love and lofty ideals of the white man." As an Indian agency doctor, he had hardly expected to attend to the victims of a massacre.

Perhaps the worst aspect of his situation was that he was a government employee working under a white agency official and was expected to side with U.S. policies on all matters, even when they went against the best interests of his people. Eastman had protested the use of force against the Ghost Dancers, but he was a physician and not a politician. Still, he found himself caught between his faith in white civilization and the interests of his people. After Wounded Knee, the two no longer seemed compatible.

Eastman's conflict over his position as an Indian working for the white man's government led to a series of quarrels between him and his bosses. Shortly after the Wounded Knee massacre, the U.S. government ordered that money should be paid to "non-hostile" Sioux as reparation for loss of life and property. But when the orders were carried out, a number of Indians at Pine Ridge complained that the money was not being distributed fairly. It was rumored that the agent in charge of making payments, as well as other government officials, were pocketing the money. Eastman lodged a complaint, but, because he did not go through the head of the Pine Ridge agency, he angered his boss. The charges were investigated and dropped.

Eastman complained that the investigation was a farce—more of a cover-up than a real attempt to address the charges—and opened up a bitter dispute between himself and agency commissioner Thomas Morgan and Indian agent George Brown, who eventually asked that Eastman be transferred to another agency. After refusing to be reassigned, Eastman was asked to resign. But Eastman's pledge to help his people went a bit further than the U.S. Indian Bureau had anticipated.

Perhaps out of disgust for the way in which the Indian Bureau had handled the Wounded Knee reparations, Eastman decided to go into private practice. But there was another, perhaps more important, consideration: his and Elaine's first child, a girl, had been born in 1892, and another child was on the way—so he also needed to be concerned with providing for his family. So, after more than 30 years' absence from his native homeland, Eastman moved to St. Paul, Minnesota, hung up a sign, and waited for patients. Although he had passed the Minnesota state licensing exam for physicians, because he was an Indian he was repeatedly charged with conducting an illegal practice. Although it was not illegal for an Indian to practice medicine, it was thought by many that, because Eastman was an Indian, he could not possibly be a qualified and licensed physician. Eastman had experienced racism before and was determined not to give in to it, and after awhile his practice began to improve, drawing increasing numbers of patients and gaining respectability. However, it wasn't long before Eastman got the itch to resume his work in the reservation system. He again applied to the government for an agency appointment in Sioux territory. An offer came not from the Indian agency, however, but from the Young Men's Christian Association (YMCA), which had recently been setting up Indian schools around the country.

The offer appealed to Eastman, as did the salary of $2,000 a year, and in 1894 he accepted. The job involved a great deal of traveling—he toured Sioux agency schools in South Dakota, North Dakota, and Nebraska, and he even visited the famous Carlisle Indian School in Carlisle, Pennsylvania. Eastman threw himself wholly into the task of establishing new schools and improving existing ones. During his tenure with the YMCA, Eastman had a great impact. He combatted alcoholism among Indians by introducing Bible study programs, and helped acquire the necessary equipment to set up agency sports competitions in baseball, lacrosse, and football. In addition, he served as secretary of the newly formed Indian Rights Association in Iowa. During his five-year stint with the YMCA, Eastman took part in setting up more than 40 Indian organizations. The best thing about this type of work for Eastman was that it brought him closer to his people. He later wrote of this period as a "wonderful opportunity to come into close contact with the [Indian] mind, and to refresh my understanding of the philosophy in which I had been trained, but which had been overlaid by a college education." The YMCA was, for Eastman, one of the "best products of American civilization."

By the mid-1890s, the Eastman family had grown to six, with the addition of three girls and a boy. And although the YMCA work was rewarding, it had two drawbacks: he was away from his family for weeks at a time, and he wasn't able to employ his skills as a physician. After resigning from the YMCA in 1899, he worked for a year as an agent for the Carlisle Indian School and continued looking for a job as an agency physician. His search ended in September, 1900, when he was named agency physician at the Crow Creek agency in South Dakota. Once again he had set himself between the Indian and white worlds. But this time Eastman was determined to stick to medicine and avoid agency politics. His first concern at Crow Creek was to inoculate the Indians against the spread of smallpox, a disease that had wiped out entire tribes in the past. But the Indians feared the side effects of the vaccination, so Eastman had to cajole and convince them to take it. In this he was very successful; the number of cases of smallpox was greatly reduced at Crow Creek, and there were no epidemics. In fact, during Eastman's stay, the birth rate exceeded the death rate at Crow Creek for the first time in more than a decade.

Although Eastman had great success in his medical work, politics once again got in the way. This time, agency commissioner Harry Chamberlain became angry with Eastman for supposedly encouraging a group of Indians who were complaining about government policies at Crow Creek. Chamberlain retaliated by filing a list of complaints against Eastman and by asking for his removal from the agency. Only one of the charges against Eastman was ever proved—an accusation of "immoral conduct" for examining women without the presence of a third party. Despite the success of Eastman's medical work, he was reassigned in 1901.

The Indian agency felt that Eastman's racial ties to the Sioux prevented him from doing his job properly. Therefore, instead of giving him another job as physician on an Indian agency, he was put in charge of renaming the Sioux. Indian names presented an obstacle to gaining citizenship—some Indians were known by numerous names, and others had names that seemed ridiculous to non-Indians. For example, names such as "Man-who-is-afraid-of horses," "Skunk's-father," and "Let-them-have-enough," besides being considered silly to the whites, gave no indication of family relations or bloodlines to outsiders. In addition, the Indians' retention of their Indian names was contrary to the intent of the Dawes Act and its citizenship provision, which aimed to assimilate Indians into white society and cut them off from tribal customs. Thus, Eastman was charged with providing the Indians with names that would make it easier for them to deal with white people—a task that he was very good at. He altered Sioux names so that they resembled Anglo-Saxon names without altering their meaning. For example, "She-who-has-a beautiful-house" became Sarah Goodhouse, and "Rotten Pumpkin" became Robert Pumpian. In about six years, Eastman gave new names to approximately 25,000 Sioux. This work also gave him a good chance to help his people achieve citizenship and secure rights to their property, something that had been a concern of his since his college days.

During this period, Eastman also moved his family back to Massachusetts, where he hoped to begin a new career—that of a writer. As agency physician and YMCA Indian secretary, and in his continuing work for the Indian Bureau, Eastman had been able to do his small part to help his people and to forward the cause of Indian rights; but as a writer, he felt he could do more. Eastman wrote on a variety of subjects, covering nearly all aspects of Sioux life and customs. In 1902 Eastman published his first book, *Indian Boyhood*, the story of his early life in a Sioux village; *From the Deep Woods to Civilization* (1916), a later book, continued the story of his life. In addition to his autobiographical works, Eastman wrote short stories, which were collected in *Old Indian Days* and *Red Hunters and the Animal People*. In *Indian Heroes and Great Chieftains*, Eastman wrote about the lives of great figures in Indian history, such as the great warrior, medicine man, and fellow Sioux, Sitting Bull, who is most famous for leading the Sioux against General George Armstrong Custer and his U.S. cavalry troops at the 1876 Battle of Little Bighorn.

The Soul of the Indian (1911), an account of Sioux religious experiences and beliefs, was one of Eastman's most ambitious works. In it, he attempted to defend the religion of his people against the widely held belief among non-Indians that Indian religion was crude, barbaric, and heathen. Eastman felt that Sioux spirituality was as lofty as that of Christianity, and that the fundamental teachings of both were essentially the same.

Eastman knew that with understanding came sympathy, and his goal in writing was to help whites understand Indian culture, and thus begin to treat Indians with the respect due them. Whatever flaws or weaknesses exist in his writing—and there are many—it must be said that he succeeded in bringing a truer

In his writings, Eastman, pictured here in traditional Sioux dress, sought to bring a greater understanding of Indian culture to the non-Indian public. (Smithsonian Institution)

picture of Native American life to public attention at a time
when Indian ways of life and customs were regarded by most
non-Indians as heathen and uncivilized. His purpose was, he
said,

> Not to entertain, but to present the American Indian in his true
> character before Americans. The barbarous and atrocious character
> commonly attributed to him has . . . led to deep demoralization.
> Really it was a campaign of education on the Indian and his true
> place in American history.

But evidently, Eastman did entertain as well as educate. His
books made him famous among the general public and the
literary community alike. He was one of the many great writers
of the period to be invited to Mark Twain's 70th birthday party.
But Eastman could not have achieved this fame without the help
of his wife, Elaine. She edited all of his early writings and is
responsible for the polish of the prose style in his books. Indeed,
she played a key role in all of Eastman's endeavors.

Sadly, Eastman's marriage slowly deteriorated. The rift between Eastman and his wife widened in the early 1910s, shortly after
they organized two summer camps, one for boys and one for girls,
in Granite Lake, New Hampshire. The reasons for their ultimate
divorce are uncertain, but the failure of these camps and resulting
financial problems may have played a part. Also, since his days
working for the YMCA, Eastman had often worked away from
home for long periods of time. Although they were not divorced
until 1920, the Eastmans were separated long before then.

During the early to mid-1910s, Eastman threw himself, body
and soul, into the politics of Indian issues. With his fame as an
author came a series of lecture tours and speaking engagements.
In these lectures, Eastman focused his discussion on the fight to
gain Indian citizenship. In 1915, Eastman was named president
of the Society of American Indians, an organization devoted to
winning citizenship for all Indians. At the close of World War I,
Eastman and his colleagues pointed out that, despite the fact
that nearly 10,000 Indians had served in the U.S. Army, they
were still denied the rights accorded all American citizens. He

also called for the abolition of the Indian Bureau, an organization that was supposed to act in the interests of Indians, but which was often plagued by corruption and mismanagement of Indian affairs. Unfortunately, the Society of American Indians, like so many good-intentioned Indian alliances, suffered from internal division and disagreement on a number of issues, and Eastman resigned from the organization in disgust in 1920.

After his divorce from Elaine and his resignation from the society, things got progressively worse for Eastman. He returned to Indian service in 1923 as an investigator of complaints, and once again had the chance to visit different Indian groups and experience their ways of life. He lived for short periods among the Chippewa in Minnesota, the Mackinac in Michigan, the Osage in Oklahoma, and the Sioux. But the fight seemed to have gone out of Eastman, or else he had learned too well what came of being overly sympathetic to Indian complaints. His investigations rarely, if ever, led to improvements in the situations on the reservations, and he failed to expose the abuses of many agency officials. Partly owing to frustration and partly as a result of failing health, Eastman resigned his inspectorship in 1925 after only two years on the job.

Eastman now supported himself, when he was not too weak from declining health, by continuing to lecture on Indian issues and to plead on behalf of Indian citizenship. On one occasion, Eastman traveled throughout England and, in traditional Sioux dress, lectured on the Indian situation back in America. But the rigors of travel and public appearances soon made this impossible, and he retired to a home he had bought in Ontario, just north of Lake Huron. Little is known of these quiet years, spent far from the Sioux country of his boyhood and outside the boundaries of the country he had embraced. It would appear that, wearied by years of hard work committed to Indian rights issues, he deliberately withdrew from the fight. Some scholars suggest that Eastman may have been writing a history of the Sioux, but the manuscript has never been found. Whatever the extent of his efforts in his later years, they came to an end in Detroit in 1939 when, at the age of 80, he died of a heart attack.

Others who took up the fight in the 20th century were proud to point to Eastman as an example of what American Indians are capable of accomplishing. From early manhood on, Eastman was held up as an example of what education could do for Indian people, and he always lived up to that reputation, both in his work as a doctor and his writings. And, not content merely to serve as an example, he never abandoned the struggle for Indian rights and citizenship. In the early 1970s, the Charles Eastman Fellowship was established by the Association of American Indian Affairs and Mead Johnson and Company to provide funding for Indian medical students. Eastman could not have wished for a better tribute. His journey "from the deep woods to civilization" remains a testament to the abilities and perseverence of Indian peoples.

ALEXANDER POSEY

◆ ◆ ◆

Creek Poet and Journalist
(1873–1908)

In many ways the life and work of Alexander Posey embodies the confusion and upheaval, the idealism and the tragedy, of late-19th-century life in Indian Territory. Posey was of mixed ancestry—he was part Creek and part white. He was progressive in the sense that he thought that Indians should join white civilization, yet he was sympathetic to the traditional ways of those who resisted progress. As an artist and a writer, Posey revered nature and respected the land, but as a businessman and land speculator he exploited the land in hopes of making a fortune. For years he was an avid supporter of statehood for Oklahoma. Then, after spending time among the traditional Creeks, he became an avid supporter of separate statehood for the Creek Nation.

If Posey was consistent in anything, it was in that he always followed his passions and never shrank from the heated issues of the day. He felt that progress was inevitable, that Indians could either change their ways and enjoy the prosperity that came with progress or fall victim to the new way. This sentiment is summed up by Chitto Harjo, one of the many fictional characters Posey created to speak from the viewpoint of the traditionally minded Creek:

> The white man he was make town and make town and build railroad and build railroad and appoint federal judge and appoint federal judge to say it was all right and we couldn't help it. So if we was had a council to talk it over, the marshal and soldiers was

arrest us for trying to kill the president and put us in jail to catch consumption and maybe so lice. So I was make a motion to give it up and see what become of us anyhow.

According to Posey, Indians had to accept progress as the better part of a bad deal—it was that or nothing. And Posey's life was one of accepting the inevitable and of trying to make the best of it.

◆ ◆ ◆

On August 3, 1873, near present-day Eufaula, Oklahoma, Hence and Nancy Posey had their first child. They named him Alexander after Alexander the Great, the world conquerer from Macedonia. Nancy was a full-blooded Creek, daughter of a Baptist minister who had come to Oklahoma after the Creek were removed from Alabama. From his mother, Posey learned about traditional Creek customs and heard the stories of his people's history. Hence's origins were largely unknown, even to himself. Although he claimed to be part Creek, he was a white orphan who was adopted and raised by a wealthy Creek family. By the time Alex came into the world, Hence was a prosperous farmer and was active in Indian government in the Tuskegee region of Oklahoma.

The Posey ranch was situated near Bald Hill in a beautiful, hilly section of eastern Oklahoma bordering on the Canadian River. The natural beauty of the region was for Alex an ideal childhood setting that would become a source for pastoral descriptions in his poetry. From being close to nature, and from his mother's teaching him about the Creek tradition of love and respect for all natural things, Posey grew to love natural landscapes. In "My Hermitage" he says,

> I ask no more of life than sunset's gold;
> A cottage hid in songbird's neighborhood,
> Where I may sing and do a little good
> For love and pleasant memories when I'm old.

In fact, he developed an emotional attachment to this region that brought him back time and time again, and he longed to have a secluded hideaway near Bald Hill.

But the peace and quiet of Bald Hill were in sharp contrast to the surrounding tumult of an Indian nation facing dissolution. The Creek were sharply divided between those who favored preserving the traditional way of life—the conservatives—and those who favored progress and American citizenship. In 1867, Creek delegates had drawn up a constitution modeled after the U.S. Constitution. While many favored adopting this document as the law of the Creek Nation, others opposed this measure. After years of bitter dispute, the two sides clashed in 1882 in what has come to be known as the Green Peach War. Hence Posey sided with the progressives and was a captain in the army that eventually defeated the anticonstitutional forces. His involvement with the progressive movement had a great deal to do with Alex's own political position.

With Hence Posey's faith in progressive ideals, there was no question that his son should learn English. Although Hence had learned to speak English while serving in the Confederate army during the U.S. Civil War, and Nancy had picked up some English, Creek was spoken at the Posey ranch. As a result, Alex was 12 before he began serious study of English. Around 1885, Alex was sent to the Creek national public school in Eufaula, Oklahoma, and he soon stood out as one of its most promising students. His favorite subject was literature, especially poetry, and he read everything he could get his hands on. He also found time after school and during vacations to work for the local newspaper, the *Indian Journal*. By the time he was 17, Alex began contributing articles to the paper.

In 1889 the Creek board of education selected 10 students to send to Bacone Indian University. Alex was one of them. Although it was called a university, Bacone had only a high-school-level curriculum. Posey delved into his studies and quickly attracted the notice of his teachers, who asked him to speak at the graduation exercises. His subject was the progress of Indian intellectual achievement, and he pointed to Sequoyah, the inventor of the Cherokee alphabet, as an example of Indian intelligence and as a sign of that progress. So impressive was Posey's speech that it was later reprinted in the *Indian Journal*. It wasn't long before his name became synonomous with the new breed of educated Indians.

All of this public attention served to fuel Posey's literary ambitions. And he was never at a loss for something to write about. From his mother, Nancy, Posey had been given a wealth of Creek stories, history, and customs that he could draw upon. From Hence he inherited a political cause, that of progress, statehood, and citizenship.

During his years at Bacone, Posey often contributed to the *Indian Journal* in Eufaula. In his articles he began to develop a key aspect of his personality—his sense of humor. Those who knew Posey often remarked about his sense of fun and his fondness for practical jokes. This lightheartedness also came out in much of his early poetry, such as in the boasts of "Wildcat Bill":

> I'm Wildcat Bill,
>   From Grizzle Hill,
> A border ranger; never down'd;
>   A western hero all around;
> A gam'ler, scalper; born a scout;
>   A tough; the man ye read about,
> From no man's lan';
>   Kin rope a bear an' ride a buck;
> Git full on booze an' run amuck;
>   Afeard o' nothin'; hard to beat;
> Kin die with boots upon my feet—
>   An' like a man!

From an early age, Posey seems to have been schooled in the devices of the folklorist, such as exaggeration, boasting, the use of dialect, and the art of the tall tale. In fact, these devices are very much a part of Creek storytelling.

In addition, Posey listened carefully to the dialect and mannerisms of traditional Creek Indians who had not been to the mission schools, and was able to copy them down. He knew where the Indian's sense of humor lay and was able to evoke laughter and lighten up a tense political situation. But most of all he knew how effective satire was as a political weapon, and he often used humor to ridicule the more traditionally minded Creeks.

In 1894, Posey decided not to return to Bacone for his final year. Instead he went into the world of business, taking a job as salesman for the Brown Brothers Company in the Seminole tribal country to the south. Whether Posey was unsuccessful as a salesman or whether he was just homesick is uncertain, but he returned home after only a year with Brown Brothers and entered Creek politics. Through Hence's connections, Posey was appointed to the House of Warriors, a governing body in the Creek Nation. Later he was made superintendent of the Creek Orphan School in Okmulgee, Oklahoma. It was at Okmulgee that Posey wrote most of his poetry. His duties there were limited, and he was left with much free time for reading and writing. Also, he surrounded himself with teachers who had literary interests, one of whom was his longtime friend, George Riley Hall.

One of the teachers Posey recruited was a young woman from Arkansas named Lowena Harris. Posey had met her earlier that year and was greatly impressed by her interest in Indian education. Her beauty and intelligence also seemed to play no small part in his hiring her. According to Lowena Harris, it was love at first sight. And the two wasted no time in, as Posey called it, "tying the knot." They were married in the spring of 1896 and settled into what was probably the happiest period of their lives. With the company of Hall, marital bliss, and the birth of a son in 1897, Posey was spurred on to great literary productivity. Scottish poet Robert Burns was Posey's favorite, and from him Posey learned that the musical quality of native dialect made for great lyric poetry. Although Posey made little use of Creek vernacular in his poetry, it played a key part in his most ambitious literary work, the "Fus Fixico Letters."

But in 1898 these blissful days at Okmulgee came to an end. George Hall was restless and found a teaching position closer to a piece of land he had bought. Posey, too, became restless. He had been dreaming of becoming a rancher like his father and had staked off some land near Bald Hill, where he had grown up. Most residents of the Creek Nation were herding and farming people, and so this way of life seemed natural to Posey. But he also felt that farming would leave him more time to devote to his writing. With the help of friends and family, Posey built a modest home and undertook the life of a farmer. This return to Bald Hill did, in fact, inspire Posey, and some of his best nature poetry was written during this period. He had found a retreat similar to the one described in one of his favorite books, *Walden*, by Henry David Thoreau. One of Posey's poems from this period reflects his feelings:

Between me and noise of strife,
The walls of mountains set with pine;
the dusty care-strewn paths of life
Lead not to this retreat of mine.

Although Posey himself was hidden away at Bald Hill, his name was not. During this period his byline, and his poems, appeared often in newspapers as distant as the Kansas City *Star*, the St. Louis *Republic*, and the New York *Evening Sun*. White readers marveled at the adept style and perceptive natural observations of the Creek poet. Information about Posey's life was printed alongside his poems, and he achieved no small bit of fame.

Instead of reveling in his growing fame, however, Posey felt that his poems were meant for the people of Oklahoma—that only the people of that region could truly appreciate them. This is perhaps why he never sought to collect and publish his work. It was not long before Posey ceased altogether to send his work out to newspapers. It was almost as though he did not want the outside world to intrude upon his quiet life as a farmer.

Just as farming was in Posey's blood, so was politics. However, it may have taken the death of his father, Hence, in 1902 to shake Posey out of his reclusive life. Or it may have been the final push of the movement for statehood and citizenship that brought him back. Either way, Posey did come out of his retreat, to become editor of the *Indian Journal* and, in the process, to give up writing poetry. As editor of the *Journal*, Posey continued to believe that only local news was of importance. This is much in evidence in his prose writings for the paper. The *Journal* stories were concerned only with local events, however mundane those events happened to be. Posey wrote articles about the huge size of a radish grown by a local farmer; about how citizens were letting the grass on their lawns get too high; and about a cow that had been wandering the streets of Eufaula. Such stories brought out the best of Posey's sense of humor.

Posey's focus on local affairs made the *Journal* very popular—so popular, in fact, that in 1902 the paper merged with the Eufaula *Gazette*. Posey also had pledged to stay neutral on matters of Creek politics, and he did, in his own way. Instead of writing opinionated

Alexander Posey became known throughout the state of Oklahoma for his sharp wit and his delightful sense of humor. (Archive and Manuscript Division of the Oklahoma Historical Society)

editorials, Posey used his skill as a satirist and as an expert on Creek dialect to get across his viewpoints. He accomplished this through the use of personae—fictional characters who could express his views without drawing attention to him as the author.

This use of personae led to what most scholars agree is Posey's most formidable literary achievement, the "Fus Fixico Letters." Fus Fixico, which means "heartless bird" in Creek, was a sort of comic strip character, a full-blooded Creek commenting on the affairs of the Creek Nation. The letters also reported remarks made by other memorable Creek personalities of Posey's creation, such as Hotgun, Wolf Warrior, Kono Harjo, and Tookpafka Micco, with Posey making extensive use of his knowledge of Creek dialect. And through the fog of crude but intelligent dialogue, Posey could get his point across, as in the following letter:

> Tookpafka Micco he go on an' say "Well, so [the statesman] tell 'em Oklahoma an' Injin Territory make a fine lookin' couple an' ought to had they picture taken together, so congress could have it enlarged an' hang it up on the map o' our common country. Then he go an' pay a glowin' tribute to the pioneers. He say they . . . was replace the wild animals with domestic ones, . . . they was chop down saplin's an' buil' huts; they was dig in the sod an' throw up rude abodes, they was laid the foundation o' a new state, an' give civilization a home in the backwoods. . . .
>
> Then Hotgun he spit over the backlog an' say, "Well, so the young statesman from the banks o' the Wabash wasn't up on facts an' ancient hist'ry. He was just puttin' words together to see how many he had. The Injin was the only bona fide pioneer in this country, an' the Injin squaw was the woman that furnish the magic an' help overcome the wild animals an' carry civilization into the waste places.
>
> An' Tookpafka Micco he smoke slow and study long time an' say, "Well, so the lord helps 'em that help 'emselves—except the Injin."

To the Creek of Oklahoma at the turn of the century, Hotgun, Tookpafka, and Chitto Harjo were not unlike Gary Trudeau's Doonesbury characters of today's Sunday comics—humorous, realistic, poignant, and widely read. The conservative Creek and the progressive Creek still had their hostilities, and the "Fus Fixico

Letters" helped to lessen the tension between the two factions. And the literary value of the letters is undeniable. Posey created characters that accurately represented the life and attitudes of tradition-minded Creeks. Although he often held the traditionalists up to ridicule, he revealed the intelligence and thoughtfulness behind their political views as well. As word of Posey's "Fus Fixico Letters" spread, papers all over the country wrote and asked to print them. Again Posey refused, as he had done with his poetry, saying that his writing was of local interest only and would not be understood elsewhere. He seemed always to shy away from national attention and fame.

Posey seemed to live in the minds of these characters, and this is perhaps why he came to reconsider his position on statehood. Soon he came to side with those Creeks who sought separate statehood and self-government. The main reason for Posey's change of heart was his growing suspicion of the 1887 Dawes Act, which called for dividing up reservation and tribal lands and alloting them in small parcels to individual Indians. The act effectively ended any sovereignty that Indian nations had had up until that time and often deprived the tribes of millions of acres that were declared "surplus" after the allotments were parceled out to whites.

The implementation of this allotment policy among other Indian tribes had left Indians vulnerable to shady land speculators and cheats. Despite this knowledge, however, many Creek favored land allotments, thinking that they should take what they could get or else they would end up with nothing. Separate statehood, on the other hand, would allow them to allot land without any U.S. government control. As Fus Fixico said, "They is lots a good land and Injins ought a grab it theyselves stead a letting government sell it cheap for spot cash like a storekeeper that think he was going get caught."

As statehood seemed more and more imminent, Posey adapted his views to the inevitable. He attended the Creek National Council in 1904, where he met J. J. Beavers, chief clerk of Creek enrollment for land allotment. Because of Posey's knowledge of the language and customs of the Creek, Beavers hired him to assist in enrollment. For the next two and a half years Posey traveled throughout the Creek Nation trying to compile a census of the Creek population so that, when statehood came, all Indians would be sure to be alloted their share of the land. In short, the more Creek he tracked down, the more land would be held by the Creek after Oklahoma was admitted into the Union. Posey took this work seriously and was very successful in recording the names of isolated people, many of whom would hide from Posey when he came around because they didn't want their names enrolled.

The Snakes, or traditional Creek, were the most resistant to enrollment. Although Posey was sympathetic with their views, he knew that they must either get an allotment or be dispossessed of their land. Therefore, he stopped at nothing in order to enroll them, at times riding 18 miles on horseback only to find that the family had run off and hidden in their cornfields.

The work was difficult and time-consuming, and the production of "Fus Fixico Letters" came to a standstill. However, the contact with the Snakes had renewed Posey's interest in Creek storytelling. He began recording the stories he heard. Unfortunately, there is no trace of these stories—they were either lost or destroyed. These stories, aside from a scant number of "Fus Fixico Letters," were to be his last literary production. Changed through his contact with the Snakes, Posey threw his support behind one last desperate move for separate statehood, called the Sequoyah movement. Posey himself signed the constitution drawn up by supporters of the Sequoyah movement, and even suggested that the separate state be called "Sequoyah," but it seemed that he knew this measure was doomed to fail. In October, 1907, Oklahoma was admitted into the Union, thereby putting into effect the Dawes Act.

Posey once again showed that he was quick to adapt to political and social change. Although he had actively opposed statehood, he was determined to make the best of the situation now, and saw his opportunity to make money in the real estate boom that was sweeping through Oklahoma. In 1907 he went to work for the International Land Company, which was owned and operated by C. M. Bradley, a businessman with a reputation for shady dealings.

It seemed that when it came to business matters Posey's moral judgment flew out the window, and with this move, his reputation and his credibility in the Creek Nation went with it. Many Creek felt that Posey had betrayed his own people. But Posey certainly believed that Indians must assert themselves and take their share of the profits. While working for Bradley, Posey also went into business for himself, joining with his friend D. P. Thornton to form the Posey-Thornton Gas Company—an oil drilling venture. Later that year Posey started working for the Palo Alto Land Company as a land agent. His job was to act as intermediary in the purchasing of land from full-blooded Creek. Records show that Posey did not make a great deal of money in this work; instead it put him deep into debt. He accumulated a lot of land, but money could only be made by resale at a higher price than what he had paid for it, and this sometimes could take years.

By applying all of his energy to business affairs, Posey left himself with little time to write. Except for the occasional article in the *Indian Journal,* Posey seems to have abandoned his literary aims. Before he ever had a chance to resume his writing or to live up to the great promise he had shown as a poet and as author of the "Fus Fixico Letters," tragedy struck. Posey had been hard at work on a test oil well near Bald Hill while Lowena and their son were in Fayetteville visiting her family. Heavy rains had pelted the Muskogee region for more than a week, and the North Canadian River, which lay between Bald Hill and Eufaula, was flooded.

On May 27, 1908, Posey was to meet with an agent from the Galbreath Oil Company in Eufaula. The level of the North Canadian River had subsided enough to allow passage, but not without some risk. Posey knew the river well and had crossed it innumerable times since he was a boy. The railroad bridge, which was the usual passage across the river, had been washed away, so Posey and his friend, Robert Howe, hired a boat and attempted a crossing. The current proved to be too rough—the boat capsized and the two men were thrown into the swirling water. Howe was able to grab a railroad tie and hoist himself up onto the riverbank, but Posey was not so lucky. He caught hold of a small tree to keep from being swept away by the current while Howe went to get a rope. But Posey's strength finally gave way and he was sucked under the railroad ties and cast headlong down the river. So devastating was the flood that nearly a month passed before his body was recovered.

News of Posey's death spread throughout Oklahoma. The tragic events surrounding his death made him an instant folk hero. Newspapers all over the country carried the story of the unfortunate demise of this "most promising of Indian writers." Although Posey was well known among the Creek in Oklahoma, his work never reached a national audience. He was never courted by the literary world, and it seemed that Posey preferred to remain a local hero. His world, like his fame, was confined to the rolling hills of eastern Oklahoma. The publication of Posey's collected poems in 1910 did little to bring him to the attention of a wider audience. However, his finest literary achievement, the "Fus Fixico Letters," were published recently in 1993. This publication should bring Posey the attention he has long deserved.

NATIVE AMERICAN ETHNOLOGISTS

◆ ◆ ◆

Caretakers of Culture

Imagine what it would be like if you no longer had a senior prom, a homecoming football game, or a graduation ceremony to look forward to. Imagine what it would be like if you no longer went trick-or-treating on Halloween, exchanged valentines on February 14th, played practical jokes on April Fool's Day, or observed religious holidays. Imagine what it would be like to see these annual rituals and ceremonies replaced by those of another culture. Since Europeans first landed in North America, the loss of such cherished cultural activities has been a reality for Native Americans.

Fortunately, many people today are concerned with preserving their ethnic heritage and keeping alive the rituals and ceremonies of their people. This chapter will explore the life and work of men who lived during a period when their cultures and their traditions were in danger of being lost forever because there was no written record of tribal ritual, language, and beliefs. Thanks to these men, people today know a great deal about Native American traditions. These men were ethnographers (professionals who record information about a culture) and ethnologists (professionals who study a culture). Often they worked for white anthropologists and, because they knew the language and customs of their people, were hired to interpret the speech of tribal elders who remembered the "old ways" and to collect information about their tribe's songs, ceremonies, rituals, and way of life. But their work was not universally appreciated. Many Native Americans were opposed to the removal of tribal artifacts from the reservations. In fact, many ethnographers were accused of thievery and of violating a sacred trust.

Although many Native American intellectuals have devoted their lives to the study of their own people, this chapter will focus on the life and work of three of the most famous Indian ethnographers: James R. Murie, Jesse Cornplanter, and John Joseph Mathews. Through years of hard work, these men helped to record and preserve the cultural life of their tribes, and they deserve to be recognized as leaders in the field of Indian ethnography.

James R. Murie

Pawnee Ethnographer
(1862–1921)

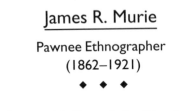

James R. Murie, along with Francis La Flesche (see page 51), was one of the first Indian ethnographers. Born in 1862 at Grand Island, Nebraska, Murie was the son of a white man and a Pawnee woman. He was given the Pawnee name *Saku rù ta'*, or "Coming Sun." At this time, Pawnee traditions and culture were very much alive. The Pawnee still lived in tipis and earthlodges and hunted buffalo. Murie was later to describe his experience of a buffalo hunt in this way:

> Once I went swimming while the men went after bufflos. while I was in the water. I seen a bufflo coming. I had to climbed upon a tree. it was mad some men were after him and had some arrows in him. they killed him and then I got down from the tree. and I seen them skin it.

Although Murie was still struggling with his new language, the letter shows that from an early age he was interested in observing and recording Indian activities. In 1879, his mother sent him to the

Hampton Institute in Virginia to improve his English. At Hampton, he came under the influence of the great African-American educator Booker T. Washington, and he joined the Episcopal Church and planned to become a minister. However, after completing his degree in four years, he returned to Nebraska to teach English to his fellow tribespeople. He was the first member of his tribe to be educated in the East.

What he found upon his return in 1883 was a world very different from the one that he had left. Instead of hunting buffalo, the Pawnee were making the transition to an agricultural way of life; instead of earthlodges, he saw log houses. During his absence, an agency school had been set up, and this is where he started his first teaching job. Thus Murie began a professional and intellectual career that, except for a brief attempt at farming, was to last until the end of his life.

After a year at the agency school, Murie took a job as an English teacher and assistant disciplinarian at the Haskell Institute in eastern Nebraska. This, too, was only temporary. Not long after he took the job at Haskell, the U.S. commissioner of Indian affairs named him to the post of official interpreter at the Pawnee agency, and he was given an office in the Tribal Community House when it was built in 1890. Through his work as interpreter, Murie became involved in tribal and agency matters, and he recorded names for the land allotments that were to be distributed when the U.S. government had achieved its goal of dissolving the Pawnee Nation and making tribe members American citizens. This process had begun in 1887 with the passing of the Dawes Act, which parceled out land to Indians provided that they became U.S. citizens. (Although under this act Indians were made citizens, their citizenship was conditional upon the individual Indian's ability to prove "competency," meaning that each individual had to make good use of the land and sever all connections to tribal organizations.)

In 1893, while performing his duties as agency interpreter, Murie had a chance meeting that was to change his life. The person he met was an anthropologist named Alice Fletcher, and she had come to study the Pawnee way of life. Fletcher's enthusiasm for her work and her fascination with Pawnee culture excited Murie.

He soon began to take an interest in the native songs and ceremonies that he had always taken for granted. Fletcher asked him to interpret traditional stories and songs; this in turn gave him a certain pride in his ethnic heritage. Fletcher's stay with the Pawnee resulted in the publication in 1904 of *The Hako: A Pawnee Ceremony.* Murie is credited in the book with having provided valuable assistance in the collection of the information that appears in it.

Fletcher's book brought Murie's name to the attention of George Dorsey, then curator of anthropology at the Field Museum of Natural History in Chicago. Dorsey, too, had taken an interest in Pawnee culture, and he did not hesitate to hire Murie as his assistant when he began his study of the tribe. Because of Dorsey's responsibilities at the Field Museum, he depended upon Murie to gather most of his data on the Pawnee. For the next six years, Murie worked as Dorsey's field researcher, recording Pawnee myths and traditions, collecting cultural items such as clothing, tools, and sacred bundles, and taking notes on ritual ceremonies. The information accumulated by Murie and Dorsey led to the publication of some six books on the Pawnee, most notable among them a two-volume study entitled *The Pawnee: Mythology* (1906).

Murie's interests, however, also branched off from Dorsey's work. In his spare time, he worked on a very ambitious study of the Pawnee language in the hope of putting together a Pawnee-English dictionary. Unfortunately, Murie never completed this work, but his effort shows that he felt strongly enough about his ethnographic skills to work independently. The Bureau of American Ethnology showed that they had confidence in Murie as well, for they hired him as an independent field researcher in 1910. The bureau also gave Murie a typewriter, a camera, and a gramophone so that he could record Pawnee songs. It was at about this time that Murie attended and took notes on the last performance of the Bear Dance of the Pitahawirata band of the Pawnee. If not for Murie's notes, the knowledge of this important ceremony would have been lost to future generations.

By this time Murie was beginning to make quite a name for himself as an ethnographer. In 1912, Clark Wissler, curator of anthropology at the American Museum of Natural History in New York, commissioned him to write a book on the various

Pawnee societies and their ceremonies and dances. During the next two years, Murie spoke with many tribal elders, observed the rituals of the various branches of the tribe, and collected objects for the museum. This work resulted in a monograph called *Pawnee Indian Societies,* which was published by the Museum of Natural History along with a shorter manuscript on the Buffalo Dance.

Thanks to James R. Murie's extensive ethnographic work, more is known about Pawnee ceremonies than about those of almost any other Native American group. (Smithsonian Institution)

Having finished *Pawnee Indian Societies*, Murie wrote to Wissler and promised him another manuscript, "a fine work—better than anything that's been done on the Indians." This work was to be the culmination of nearly 20 years of research on Pawnee life. Murie spent the remainder of his life working on this labor of love, simply titled *Ceremonies of the Pawnee*. In November 1921, Murie presented the manuscript to a very impressed Wissler, who immediately arranged to have Murie deliver a series of lectures and show films at the museum. It was to be Murie's great moment of public acclaim. However, sadly, Murie fell ill and died later that month.

Unfortunately, Murie's book has yet to be published, although many have tried to get the book into circulation. Recently, Pawnee scholar Douglas R. Parks has been editing the manuscript of *Ceremonies of the Pawnee* for publication. Perhaps the publication of this book will finally allow Murie's contribution to Indian studies to be fully appreciated.

Jesse Cornplanter

Seneca Ethnographer
(1889–1957)

◆ ◆ ◆

To look at the life and career of Jesse Cornplanter is to learn that ethnological study requires more than just hours of research, observation, and recording of data. Cornplanter's life shows that there is an important place for showmanship, and that traditional ceremonies are best understood through the art of performance. Through Jesse Cornplanter's efforts, ethnologists were able to do more than read about traditional Seneca culture—they could see it in action.

Cornplanter was born in the Seneca Nation's Newtown Longhouse in Chemung County, New York in 1889. His father, Edward Cornplanter, was of the Wolf Clan, a prominent clan in Seneca Society, and his mother, Nancy Jack, belonged to the Snipe Clan. Cornplanter was born into what one might call a show business family. From almost the moment he could walk, Jesse joined in the sacred dances of the Seneca. His father taught him all of the songs and speeches of his people, telling him never to let the ancient ceremonies pass away. In fact, the performance of Seneca ceremonies was the Cornplanters' primary means of livelihood when Jesse was growing up. His father traveled in an Indian roadshow, dancing and singing for whomever would pay him.

Although there was never very much money to be made in this kind of work, Jesse joined his father's show when he was 15. He toured England, Holland, and Germany in 1904. Cornplanter credits this trip with educating him in the ways of the white world—an education he could not have received at the local school, which he left before completing the fifth grade. Later, in 1912, he went back on tour with the celebrated "Hiawatha Show," a production based on Henry Wadsworth Longfellow's poem, "Song of Hiawatha." The show ran for nearly a year and was very popular in some southern cities, where it was often held over for weeks at a time.

But Cornplanter also had talents in other areas—drawing and illustration. He had shown artistic ability at a young age and had developed something of a reputation as a child artist. This fame led to a commission to illustrate historian Frederick Starr's *Indian Games and Dances* in 1903. Cornplanter often drew pen-and-ink sketches of deer, cornhusk dolls, and other figures in the margins of his letters, and his artistic ability provided him with a source of some income, through the sale of his illustrations of Seneca False Faces—ceremonial masks made of wood.

Shows and artwork, however, did not bring in enough money to live on. When Cornplanter and Lucinda Lay (Yáhsin) whom he had married in 1912, had their first child, the family needed to find a more reliable source of income. In 1916, Cornplanter found work in an automobile factory in Toledo, Ohio, and moved there with his wife and child. But at that time, World War I was raging in Europe, and it was only a matter of time before the United States joined the fight. Like many other Americans, Cornplanter was caught up in the patriotic fervor that swept the country, and he enlisted in 1917. While serving in France, Cornplanter was brought down by a German gas canister and had to be sent to a field hospital. He recovered in time to join the final push by the Allied forces at the end of the war.

When the time came to return home, Cornplanter found his readjustment to everyday life difficult. Both his father and his mother had died in his absence. To make matters worse, the gas had done permanent damage to his lungs, and he often needed to stay at the veterans' hospital for treatment. His breathing problems also prevented Cornplanter from playing his favorite game, lacrosse. His disability did not prevent him from participating in other aspects of his culture, however. He moved onto the Allegany reservation in western New York, one of few remaining centers of Seneca culture at the time, with a new zest for the ways of his people. His skill as a showman soon made him the focus of campfire dances and singing.

Cornplanter's career as an ethnologist appears to have begun in 1928, when he met with J. N. B. Hewitt, a well-respected ethnologist at the Bureau of American Ethnology. After the meeting, Cornplanter became interested in preserving Seneca culture in much the same way that Hewitt was working to record the lifeways of the Tuscarora tribe, which, along with the Seneca, the Cayuga, the Onondaga, the Oneida, and the Mohawk, made up the ancient and once-powerful Iroquois Confederacy. In the 1930s, Cornplanter, who had been meeting regularly with a group of tribal elders, began working with William Fenton, a Mohawk ethnologist. He and Fenton gave a talk on Seneca ceremonies at the Rochester Museum, then headed by scholar Arthur C. Parker, a Seneca Indian. Also with Fenton, Cornplanter attended Seneca ceremonies and acted as interpreter—translating Seneca into English and explaining the meaning of the ceremony.

Through Parker, Cornplanter was hired as a researcher and collector of artifacts for the Rochester Museum. This work not only provided him with a regular income; it also freed him to do something he had been planning since his meeting with Hewitt— write his own book on the Seneca. Encouraged by Fenton to write his manuscript in the form of letters, Cornplanter drew on his childhood experiences and on his own family history, and he interspersed personal facts with traditional Seneca stories. The result was *Legends of the Longhouse*, which came out in 1938. The

Jesse Cornplanter, the Seneca ethnographer and performer, appears here in traditional dress. (Photograph courtesy of William H. Fenton and the American Philosophical Society)

book was a minor success, and many of Cornplanter's friends helped to publicize it. Carl Carmer, who had written a popular book on the western New York Frontier, *Listen for a Lonesome Drum* (1936), wrote an introduction to the book. Another friend, Mrs. Walter Henricks, a Penn Yan, New York native who was devoted to the preservation of central New York Indian culture, helped to get Cornplanter's book published. The letters in the book are addressed to Henricks, who was known to the Seneca as the "White Sister."

Although Cornplanter was now a published author and had gained a bit of fame, he quickly began work on a second book. This time, however, his writing did not proceed as smoothly. He found himself repeating the same stories he had used in his first book—stories that it had taken him years to learn. To learn more would mean years of work. Cornplanter decided to set aside his second book and turn his interests once again to collecting Seneca objects and artifacts for the Rochester Museum. The main goal of his search was to retrieve sacred Seneca wampum—belts made from strands of beads that had messages woven into them. These messages were used by the Seneca and other tribes as money and as records of treaties, contracts, declarations of war, and events in tribal history. Many strands of the Seneca wampum had been lost or destroyed. Working closely with several archaeologists who had been excavating the sites of old Seneca settlements, Cornplanter was able to restore a considerable number of the strands of the Seneca wampum to the Newtown Longhouse. This work might be considered Cornplanter's greatest ethnological achievement.

Cornplanter's health worsened in the 1940s. Heart trouble caused him to slow his work, and he had to abandon many projects. However, one project, a project very dear to Cornplanter, was not abandoned. With the help of Fenton, who procured a tape recorder, Cornplanter began recording Seneca songs, chants, and speeches. Although he did not like performing without an audience, Cornplanter nevertheless produced an invaluable oral text of Seneca culture, thereby preserving it for future generations.

For the remaining years of his life, despite declining health, Cornplanter continued to participate in the ceremonies of the Seneca Longhouse—the Midwinter festivals at Newtown, Coldspring, and Tonawanda. He died on March 18, 1957, and was buried in the traditional way of the Seneca with the full rites of the Longhouse.

John Joseph Mathews

Osage Ethnologist
(1895–1979)

◆ ◆ ◆

In 1929, John Joseph Mathews had an unusual experience while traveling in North Africa. He watched in fear from his tent as a group of Arab men sped by on horses and fired their guns into the air. But then he remembered a similar encounter with young

Indian warriors when he was a boy growing up in the Osage Nation. He no longer was afraid, knowing as he did that this was "joy shooting, just joy." This experience in Africa changed his life. As Mathews put it, "I got homesick, and I thought, what am I doing over here? Why don't I go back and take some interest in my people? Why not go back to the Osage?"

Mathews did go back to the Osage, back to where his life had begun some 35 years earlier, back to Pawhuska, Oklahoma—the heart of the Osage Nation. Mathews was born November 16, 1895, son of an Osage man and a woman of French descent. The Osage were a very prosperous people, primarily because they possessed oil-rich land. During the 1890s, for instance, every Osage man, woman, and child received an annual payment of about $200—a great deal of money at the time. In addition to this income, the Mathews family also made money from their store. The young Mathews worked as a clerk in the store, where he met and befriended a number of elder full-blooded Osage—typically the more conservative branch of the nation. He in turn would ride out to visit these people and attend their dances.

Mathews grew up in a unique position in that he could experience both the traditional and modern aspects of Osage culture. But although Mathews was very interested in Osage traditions as a boy, he gradually distanced himself from these traditions as he got older. He left the Osage Nation in 1912, at the age of 18, to attend the University of Oklahoma, but his studies there were interrupted by the outbreak of World War I in 1914. Mathews joined the cavalry at first, but then, in response to his strong desire for adventure, transferred to the Air Corps and flew missions over France. After the war, he returned to the university and finished his degree in geology. But Mathews had a feeling that his education was still incomplete, so he enrolled at Oxford University in England to study natural science. This was made financially possible by a boom in the oil industry during the early 1920s and by the distribution of a portion of these profits among the Osage.

Mathews's departure for England in 1920 was only the beginning of what would be nearly a decade of wandering. After finishing his degree at Oxford, Mathews studied international relations at the University of Geneva in Switzerland, and he also worked briefly as a journalist, covering the meetings of the League of Nations in Geneva for the *Philadelphia Ledger*. From Geneva, Mathews's restless wandering took him to France, Western Europe, Scotland, and finally North Africa. He even tried his hand at real estate speculation in California. Until that fateful experience in Africa, Mathews said of himself, "I was aimless. I didn't know what I wanted. I wasn't too proud of myself." If there was one good thing about his wandering, it was that it allowed him at various times to pursue his interests in natural science, geology, and archaeology, all the while sharpening his powers of observation and inquiry. This training was to be of immense value in the work that lay ahead.

Mathews's return to Oklahoma in 1929 seemed to come not a moment too soon. When he reached Pawhuska, he found that the boom times of the Roaring Twenties had greatly affected the Osage Nation. A great number of white merchants had moved into Pawhuska to take advantage of the Osage's oil money, and many of them were involved in one way or another with the sale of liquor. Mathews found that the old way of life was nearly gone. He visited with the tradition-minded elders, who told him that they "were afraid that their mocassin prints would be washed by the sheetwaters of oblivion." They told Mathews that they wanted "to live in word symbols," meaning that they wanted to have their traditions and culture preserved and recorded in the language of white people. The elders were pleased to hear that this was the very reason for which Mathews had come home—to write the first book on the Osage.

The volume *Wah'Kon-Tah: The Osage and the White Man's Road*, published in 1932, was a reworking by Mathews of former Osage Indian agent Laban Miles's diaries. Much to Mathews's surprise, his work was named a Book-of-the-Month Club selection and sold almost 50,000 copies. This success gave Mathews, then still an unexperienced writer, the encouragement he needed. He published a novel entitled *Sundown* in 1935; *Talking to the Moon*, a book on the Osage view of the environment, in 1945; and a biographical work, *Life and Death of an Oilman: The Career of E. W. Marland*, in 1951.

But during these years of minor celebrity Mathews remained dedicated to his dream of preserving Osage culture. After his election to the Osage Tribal Council in 1934, Mathews worked to establish an Osage Tribal Museum. But many Osage took little interest in the project, and it was hard to persuade tribe members to contribute the artifacts and relics needed to fill the museum. In fact, Mathews had to make a deal with the Smithsonian Institution to borrow materials for the museum until he could collect some on his own. He then set about traveling through the Osage Nation to collect museum pieces.

While on his collecting trips, Mathews, using a tape recorder, captured for the first time an oral history that had previously only existed in the minds and mouths of the Osage. It was Mathews's dream to write all of these stories down in one great book, a book about the Osage spoken by the Osage. Mathews's approach to this book was unconventional. According to Indian scholar Garrick Bailey, Mathews relied on his training in natural science, with its close attention to detail and extensive gathering of data, in writing his history of the Osage. As Mathews described it, his method was like that of an archaeologist:

> I had bones from every part of the skeleton. More than that, when covering the finally reproduced skeleton with flesh and hide, I could use the material of my personal experiences and the experiences of my father and grand-fathers, and I, myself, had seen the dinosaur walking.

And because Mathews wanted his book to be written from the Osage point of view, with events interpreted by the Osage, he used non-Indian history sparingly and with caution. That is, when consulting a non-Indian record of Osage history as a source for information, Mathews was careful to consider the political, religious, and social interests that lay behind the author's perspective. Although many historians might argue with Mathews's methods and with his extensive use of myth, few could complain about the results of his efforts.

In 1961, after nearly 30 years of research and writing, Mathews published *The Osage*—a monumental, 788-page book that covered

John Joseph Mathews helped to preserve the cultural artifacts of his people and founded the Osage Tribal Museum. (Courtesy of the Osage Tribal Museum)

everything from the events of Osage history to tribal mythology, the lives of great chiefs and warriors, and the rites of ancient religious ceremonies. In a time when much of Osage culture was in danger of disappearing, when stories that had been told for hundreds, perhaps thousands of years were being heard by fewer and fewer Osage children, Mathews had made sure that Osage culture would not go the way of the dinosaur. Having completed his great work, Mathews devoted most of the remainder of his life to the Osage Tribal Museum. He moved into a house not far from the museum in Pawhuska, and would walk to and from the museum every day until his death on June 11, 1979.

◆ ◆ ◆

James R. Murie, Jesse Cornplanter, and John Joseph Mathews are just three American Indians who have devoted their lives to the preservation of their cultural heritage. Credit is also due to others who have followed in their footsteps, including ethnologists such as George Bushotter (Santee Sioux), William Beynon (Tsimshian), Bill Shakespeare (Arapaho), Arthur C. Parker (Seneca), and many more. Because of their special status as people who know intimately the language and customs of their own people, American Indian ethnologists have provided information that would otherwise not have been accessible to non-Indian anthropologists, and thanks to them, people today have a very good understanding and appreciation of Indian cultures.

But their contributions do not stop there. Native American scholar Margot Liberty has said that the work of ethnologists has been a tremendous help in achieving Indian reform, thereby improving the conditions of reservation life and giving many Native Americans opportunities that were not available to them in the past. When we read about Indian history and culture, when we go to a museum and see Indian artifacts, when we enjoy reading tribal myths or listening to native songs, we do well to remember the Native American ethnologists who kept these things from vanishing.

N. SCOTT MOMADAY

◆ ◆ ◆

Kiowa Author and Poet
(1934–   )

There are on the way to Rainy Mountain many landmarks,
many journeys in the one.

—N. Scott Momaday,
The Way to Rainy Mountain (1969)

No one can tell the life of N. Scott Momaday better than N. Scott Momaday, and all of Momaday's works speak in some way of his own life—a life that he feels is tied to his Indian ancestry and the stories that surround it. Momaday sees his life as a story within a story—the story of one man in the history of a people, the Kiowa. "I am a Kiowa and I shall die a Kiowa," says Momaday. When he tells of his life, he does so imaginatively, and weaves Indian mythology, ritual, and tribal memory into the fabric of personal experience.

If you were to ask Momaday how life began for him, it is likely he would answer that it began in a hollow log:

> You know, everything had to begin, and this is how it was: the Kiowas came one by one into the world through a hollow log. They were many more than now, but not all of them got out. There was a woman whose body was swollen up with child, and she got stuck in the log. After that, no one could get through, and that is why the Kiowas are small in number. They looked all around and saw the

world. It made them glad to see so many things. They called themselves *Kwuda,* "the coming out people."

—from *The Way to Rainy Mountain*

◆ ◆ ◆

Navarro Scott Momaday emerged from the hollow log in the Kiowa and Comanche Indian hospital in Lawton, Oklahoma, on February 27, 1934. There to welcome him into the world were his Kiowa father, Alfred, and his mother, Natachee, who is of Cherokee descent. Momaday's Kiowa name, *Tsoai-talee,* which means "Rock Tree Boy," refers to a sacred place in Kiowa mythology, the Devil's Tower—a 200-foot-high rock butte in Wyoming. According to Kiowa legend, a boy and his seven sisters were playing one day when, suddenly, the boy turned into a bear. The bear then chased the seven sisters . . .

> They came to the stump of a great tree, and the tree spoke to them. It bade them climb upon it, and as they did so it began to rise into the air. The bear came to kill them, but they were just beyond its reach. It reared against the tree and scored the bark all around with its claws. The seven sisters were borne into the sky, and they became the stars of the Big Dipper.
>
> —from *The Way to Rainy Mountain*

Momaday truly believes that there is something of the bear in him. Hearing such wonderful and beautiful stories as these as a child can certainly help in the development of a great writer. But Momaday was also born into a well-educated family, a family proud of its Indian heritage yet determined not to have their son's life experience limited to an Indian reservation. Alfred, an artist and educator, attended Bacone College and the universities of New Mexico and California. He began his artistic career by painting scenes from Kiowa mythology, and he was the illustrator for Momaday's book on Kiowa legend, *The Way to Rainy Mountain.* Natachee attended Haskell Institute, Crescent Girls' College, and the University of New Mexico. She studied journalism and art, wrote short stories and poetry, and also painted. Thus, from the beginning, Momaday seemed destined to become an artist.

From the time Momaday was two years old until he turned nine, his parents moved a great deal, holding teaching positions at various schools on the Navajo Reservation (located mainly in Arizona). Momaday has said that the experience of living in so many different places while growing up was an important part of his education. He learned a great deal about Navajo culture from living on the reservation and from attending Navajo schools.

The summers of his boyhood were spent with his grandparents in Oklahoma, where he listened to Kiowa stories. Momaday remembers his grandmother as having a "reverence for the sun, a holy regard that now is all but gone out of mankind." In 1887, she had taken part in the last Sundance, a ritual that celebrated the regeneration of life and the return of the buffalo to Kiowa hunting grounds. (The Kiowa stopped performing the ritual because there were no more buffalo in their territory.)

But white American culture also played an important part in Momaday's childhood experience. The first book Momaday remembers reading was *Smoky, the Cowhorse,* a cowboy book by Will James. Afterward, he read every Will James book he could get his hands on. Momaday was also a big football fan, and he confesses that as a teenager he was in love with movie star Elizabeth Taylor. But perhaps the most lasting effect non-Indian American culture has had on Momaday is his interest in the legend of Billy the Kid, the famous outlaw whose history he has incorporated into some of his writing.

The schools that Momaday attended gave him a very diverse educational background. In addition to Navajo schools, he attended several Catholic schools, a public school in Hobbs, New Mexico, and ultimately graduated from Augusta Military Institute in Virginia. Of all the places Momaday lived as a boy, his favorite was Jemez Pueblo, which sits about 30 miles east of Albuquerque, New Mexico. The beautiful desert canyons, stone houses, and vast landscape, and the traditional tribal life of the people of this region, had a lasting effect on him. At Jemez, Momaday also witnessed poverty and alcoholism, and the tension between Catholicism and traditional religious practices that continues to make life difficult for many Indians.

After graduating from military school, Momaday returned to the Southwest to attend the University of New Mexico. Although he majored in political science, Momaday retained his early interest in literature and writing. Because the university owned many important artifacts relating to English novelist and poet D. H. Lawrence, who had lived on a ranch in Taos, New Mexico, Momaday became well-acquainted with Lawrence's work during his time there.

Momaday's next educational move, to the University of Virginia, brought him into contact with a writer who was to have an even stronger influence on him. While attending Virginia's law school, he had a chance meeting with American novelist William Faulkner, who gave a reading to the Jefferson Debating Society, of which Momaday was a member. Momaday once said in an interview that Faulkner was a certified genius and that "his voice [was] very much a part of my hearing. . . . But I hope my writing is less [difficult to read] than his." Although Momaday shrugs off comparisons between his and Faulkner's writing, his patchwork narrative technique and concern for storytelling owes much to the Nobel Prize–winning author of *The Sound and the Fury*.

In 1957, Momaday left the University of Virginia without finishing his law degree, apparently deciding that the legal profession was not for him. He returned to New Mexico and found a teaching position at the Dulce Independent School on the Jicarilla Apache Reservation. Here his studies of rhetoric and language were put to good use in training Apache schoolchildren to speak English proficiently. Momaday remembers his stay at Dulce as a happy and productive period in his life:

> It was a great experience. I think I grew a lot in that year's time. I was in a very fortunate position. Well away from distraction and temptation. Lots of time in which to write, and I used it well.

Although Momaday became very attached to Dulce during his stay there, the urge to become a writer was too strong for him. He had been writing poetry since the age of nine and was now seriously considering pursuing it full time. Momaday sent a sample of his poetry along with an application for the Wallace Stegner Creative Writing Scholarship at Stanford University. For Momaday, his chances of winning the scholarship must have seemed very small. Although he had read widely, he had no formal training in writing poetry. Furthermore, some of the best young poets in the country would be competing for the chance to be instructed by Yvor Winters, one of the most distinguished poets and poetry critics of the 20th century. Winters himself judged the applications, read the poetry, and selected the person he thought had the most potential. In "recognition of his respect for, control of, and enjoyment in using language," Winters chose Momaday.

One of the poems that Momaday sent to Winters was called "Earth and I Gave You Turquoise," a poem about the death of a Navajo woman. It was to be Momaday's first published poem and was later included in his first book of poetry, *Angle of Geese and Other Poems* (1974). Momaday once said that his relationship with Winters was a "star-crossed kind of coming together—a destined meeting." Winters was perhaps the best mentor Momaday could have hoped for. Not only was he an expert on the craft of poetry; he had a special interest in American Indian poetry. Winters first began reading Indian poetry while recovering from tuberculosis in Santa Fe, New Mexico. Here Winters was also introduced to Pueblo culture, which was very much a part of Momaday's early life. As Momaday later reported, Yvor Winters "understood my ethnic and cultural background very well."

Shortly after Momaday's arrival at Stanford—a prestigious university located about 30 miles south of San Francisco—Winters took the young poet under his wing. Winters saw great potential in Momaday and was determined not to let his talents go to waste. Under Winters, Momaday received a thorough but unorthodox education in poetic form and history. Often it was Winters's habit to champion minor poets and denounce famous ones. Thus, Momaday spent a lot of time reading poets not ordinarily read by students of literature. One of these minor poets, Frederick God-dard Tuckerman, a favorite of Winters's, was to be Momaday's topic for his Ph.D. dissertation.

Winters also trained Momaday to use images in his poetry that describe in an abstract manner what is perceived by the senses. The poetry that accomplished this was the kind that Winters most ad-mired. Although Momaday later broke away from these guidelines, Winters's influence on Momaday's life and work is enormous. Speaking of his mentor, Momaday has said, "You meet someone in your life who sees you for what you are and who advises you, who stands in a position to change your life." During the next few years, as Momaday developed his own distinct writing style, Winters continued to advise him on his work. But in 1968, on the eve of his star pupil's first great literary success, Winters died.

After receiving a Ph.D. in English literature from Stanford in 1963, Momaday accepted a teaching position at the University of California at Santa Barbara. Here Momaday continued to pursue his ambition of becoming a successful poet. However, he also returned to a project he had first started at Stanford—a long narrative poem called "House Made of Dawn." This time, however, he decided to write it in the form of a novel. Momaday had a strong desire to portray Native American consciousness in a powerful way. In this endeavor, Momaday exerted great care and patience, often putting the project aside for months on end.

At this time, Momaday was dividing his time between teaching, studying American poetry, and preparing a collection of Kiowa myths. He won a Guggenheim Fellowship in 1966 that enabled him to research New England poetry. The result was Momaday's first book manuscript, a study entitled *The Furrow and the Glow: Science and Landscape in American Poetry, 1836–1866*. Unfortunately, the book was never published. The reason for this was probably that Momaday had finally put the finishing touches on his novel. And it is easy to see how the publication of *House Made of Dawn* made other projects seem somehow less important.

House Made of Dawn tells the story of Abel, a young Navajo man caught between the traditional ways practiced on the reservation and those of the modern world outside the reservation. After he returns home from the army following the end of World War II, Abel's life gradually worsens. Unable to find anything worthwhile in life, Abel drinks heavily, has an affair with a married white woman, commits a murder for no apparent reason, and is carted off to jail. After being released from jail, Abel tries living off the reservation. In Los Angeles, he meets the Priest of the Sun, who resembles Momaday in many ways—he is highly intelligent, articulate, well-read, and a Kiowa. In fact, the Priest of the Sun's monologue is one of the most powerful sections in *House Made of Dawn*, and it reveals Momaday's own concern for the oral literary tradition of Native Americans and for language in general:

> My Grandmother was a storyteller; she knew her way around words. She never learned to read and write, but somehow she knew the good of reading and writing; she had learned how to listen and delight. She had learned that in words and in language, and there only, could she have whole and consummate being. . . .
> "Storytelling; to utter and to hear" . . . When she told me those old stories something strange and good and powerful was going on.

But the Priest of the Sun fails to revive Abel's pride in his heritage or in his future. Abel gets a good job but stops going to it. He has another affair with a white woman but abandons her. Life goes on without meaning for him, and he and other Indian friends get drunk every night. After being robbed by a policeman, Abel returns to get revenge but is beaten nearly to death. He then returns to the reservation—no doubt to finish his life alcoholic, unemployed, and a ward of the state.

House Made of Dawn is as difficult to understand as it is beautifully written. Although praise for the novel was overwhelming, few critics have been able to pin down what the book "means," and it continues to give trouble to readers. Momaday's storytelling technique, his manner of using a number of different narrators, and his flashing back between present and past communicates in a powerful way what it is like to be caught between two worlds: the Indian and the white, the reservation and white society, traditional life and contemporary life, Indian religious practices and Catholicism. All of the confusion of such a difficult situation can be felt in *House Made of Dawn*. But at the same time Momaday reminds us that much of the beauty of traditional life, of who we are and where we came from, is preserved in Indian culture but absent elsewhere in the world. And perhaps the greatest achievement of *House Made of Dawn* is that it shows the complexity of American Indian life—a life that is neither completely sad nor completely happy. But even the praise of the critics paled in comparison to what followed.

In 1969, for the first time in history, a Pulitzer Prize—the most prestigious literary award given in the United States—was won by an Indian, N. Scott Momaday. It was a moment of great pride, not only for the Kiowa, but for all Native Americans. And fellow Indians were quick to honor Momaday, naming him the "Outstanding Indian of the Year." The Kiowa rewarded him by making him a member of the Gourd Dance Society, one of the highest honors that can be given to a Kiowa. In Momaday's words, this is what happens at a Gourd Dance:

> It's in Oklahoma in July. It's apt to be very humid and very hot and we wear blankets. But once the movement starts and the drum starts gathering momentum, reaching a certain pitch, you get deep into the motion of the dance, and that feeling is indescribable. It's wonderful. . . . I know why those warriors danced before they went out on raiding expeditions. It is a great way to gather yourself up, and you feel very much alive.

Rather than rest on his laurels, Momaday continued to work on collecting and adapting Kiowa myths into a single, continuous story. That summer Momaday published this collection under the name *The Way to Rainy Mountain,* with illustrations by his father. This fascinating and unique book combines traditional Kiowa stories, personal reflections, scientific observations, and historical facts concerning the Kiowa. Momaday gives equal weight to all of these sources of meaning, blending them and patching them together in such a way that they create a history of a people like no other ever written. Fact, fiction, and the individual each contribute to its making. Unlike *House Made of Dawn, The Way to Rainy Mountain* dwells on Indian fortune rather than misfortune. And the source of Indian fortune is a rich oral tradition recounting who they are and where they came from.

With Momaday's literary success came academic success as well. In 1970, he taught at the University of California at Berkeley. While there, he tried his hand at political writing, producing articles that called for protection of the American wilderness. In 1972, Momaday returned to teach at his alma mater, Stanford University, only to leave shortly thereafter for a post at New Mexico State University, where he was made distinguished visiting professor of humanities. At New Mexico State, Momaday met renowned southwestern photographer David Muench and with him produced a unique photo-poetic journey through the state of Colorado.

In the fall of 1973, Momaday again returned to teach at Stanford, only to leave at the end of the term when he was made visiting professor of American literature at the University of Moscow in what was then the Soviet Union. Here Momaday found that his students were very much interested in his Indian heritage. While teaching in Moscow, Momaday finally began to put together his first book of poetry, and his stay proved to be very productive. He wrote a great deal of poetry, and he also began to try his hand at painting. While growing up he had watched his father paint and had learned a great deal from him, and from other artists who visited his father. But he had never seriously considered expressing himself in that medium up to this point. By the late 1970s, painting was to consume more of his creative energy than either poetry or prose.

Although Momaday had been writing poetry for nearly 20 years, most of his work in verse, aside from a handful of poems he had sent to journals, had never seen the light of day. Finally, in 1974, he saw the publication of *Angle of Geese and Other Poems*. Much of the poetry reveals the influence of Yvor Winters, often containing a series of abstract observations and images. However, some poems show a departure from the ideas of his mentor, offering a more concise and straightforward treatment of Indian themes. A good example of Momaday's new style is "The Fear of Bo-talee":

> Bo-talee rode easily among his enemies, once, twice, three—and
> four times. And all who saw him were amazed, for he was utterly
> without fear; so it seemed. But afterwards he said: Certainly I was
> afraid. I was afraid of the fear in the eyes of my enemies.

In 1976, Momaday published his first major collection of poetry, *The Gourd Dancer*. The poems included in this book, among which are many poems from *Angle of Geese*, from his master's thesis, and those written in Moscow, show that Momaday's poetic production had all but ceased. And the volume received very little critical attention. It seems that, because of the success of *House Made of Dawn*, Momaday has been known primarily as a novelist, despite the tremendous amount of time and energy that he puts into his verse. Even critics who have taken the time to read his poetry seem to be of the opinion that Momaday is at his best when writing in prose.

Perhaps taking a hint from the critics, Momaday returned to prose, but not to prose fiction. Instead, he wrote about himself in a book he called *The Names: A Memoir*. *The Names* tells about what it is like to grow up Indian in America, how ancient stories and the spirits of ancestors give childhood an almost magical hue. It is also about language, about the significance of the names of people and the names that people give to things, both of which are creative acts:

> Pohd-lohk spoke, as if telling a story, of the coming-out people,
> of their long journey. He spoke of how it was that everything
> began, of Tsoai, and of the stars falling or holding fast in strange
> patterns on the sky. And in this, at last, Pohd-lohk affirmed the
> whole life of the child in a name, saying: Now you are, Tsoia-talee
> (Rock Tree Boy).

Like *The Way to Rainy Mountain*, *The Names* takes a very positive, hopeful view of Indian life. The book also tells us a great deal about the experiences that made Momaday want to become a writer, such as hearing Kiowa stories and being instilled with a strong belief in the supernatural and the mystical. With such a value placed on language and imagination, Momaday listened and learned.

The Names once again attests to the beauty of Momaday's writing. One critic called it "the Indian *Roots*"—referring to the Alex Haley novel and popular television series about an African-American writer's search for his African heritage. Another critic remarked that *The Names* is a beautiful testimony to the fact that Indians *do* live happy lives, whether on or off the reservation. Despite this praise, *The Names* did not match the success of *House Made of Dawn*. In fact, Momaday has said that he wishes he hadn't become famous so early in his career: "It was all on the basis of that one book, and when I did win the prize, it placed pressure on me. I thought, what do I do now?" Of all the burdens that came with sudden fame, the heaviest of all for Momaday was the assumption that he was some kind of spokesperson for American Indians. This was something that Momaday had never intended.

This assumption may explain Momaday's withdrawal from publishing anything fictional until 1989. In the meantime, Momaday remained very much in the public eye. In the late 1970s he had become famous enough to have his work translated into several languages, including Russian, Polish, German, Japanese, and Italian. In 1979 Momaday's writing was honored in Italy, where he was awarded the *Premio Letterario Internazionale*. Also, Momaday engaged in one of his greatest loves—travel (he is quick to remind you that the Kiowa always moved around a lot, and that that restlessness is in his blood). His successful writing career has enabled him to give readings and lectures all over the world. As Momaday scholar Charles Woodard has remarked, "Momaday is a physical and philosophical traveler, a nomad whose life is movement and whose art is a steady progression through time and place to the origins that define him and his people."

In recent years, however, Momaday has settled down to some extent and has been a professor of English at the University of Arizona, Tucson, since 1982. He has continued to paint and has had his artwork exhibited at the Museum of the American

N. Scott Momaday, winner of the Pulitzer Prize and member of the Kiowa Gourd Dance Society, at home in Arizona. (Courtesy of The University of Arizona)

Indian in New York City. He has also settled comfortably into family life. Momaday has four daughters, three from his first marriage and one with his second wife, Regina Heitzer, a native of Germany. And the raising of daughters, Momaday says, has helped him in his writing:

> Children remind us of how we saw the world at one time, and then we stop and catch our breath and understand that those ways of seeing the world are still very good. In the process of time and experience, we tend to lose our freshness of vision, and children bring it back to us.

Since the publication of *The Way to Rainy Mountain*, it is clear that Momaday has favored looking at the world through the eyes of the child. His dominant theme has been the experience of growing up as an American Indian, and he returned once again to this theme in his second novel. Twenty years after the huge success of *House Made of Dawn*, Momaday finally wrote a second novel, *The Ancient Child* (1989). *The Ancient Child* is about the struggle of an Indian artist to find and express himself. Once again Momaday's work drew critical praise. But this did not stop him from telling a *Los Angeles Times* reporter in 1989, "I don't think of myself as a novelist, I'm a poet." In a recent book, *In the Presence of the Sun* (1992), Momaday returns to poetry, yet he is masterful in the way he combines all of his talents as a poet, prose writer and artist. Momaday's search for himself and for his Indian identity continues to produce beautiful and revealing works of art. But it seems unlikely that he is or ever will be sure of who or what he is. Or, as the biographical note at the end of his new book suggests, maybe he *is* sure . . .

> He walks long distances and he rides an Appaloosa named "Ma'am." At his best he cooks. He is justly famous for a recipe named "The Washita Crossing Soup," the ingredients of which are, in his words, "simple, sacred, and secret." He is a bear.

"COMPANIONS THROUGH EVERY PAGE"

◆ ◆ ◆

Michael Dorris:
Modoc Writer, Teacher, and Scholar
(1945–   )
Louise Erdrich:
Chippewa Novelist and Poet
(1954–   )

It is late in the summer of 1985. Louise Erdrich, Michael Dorris, and their children are packing up the car for a drive from New Hampshire to Northfield, Minnesota. The children—Adam, Sava, Madeleine, Persia and Pallas—pile into the back seat and the car pulls out of the driveway. All appearances suggest that this is the beginning of the sort of family vacation that many Americans take each summer. However, this family is different. The father is a famous professor of Native American studies and is researching a book about the Sioux, and the mother is an award-winning novelist and poet.

The long drive across the country will be a productive one for the two writers. In fact, Erdrich and Dorris often discuss ideas for stories while driving long distances. The landscape, especially the broad, windswept plains of the Midwest, feeds their imagination. And this trip is no exception. Along the way, Erdrich and Dorris discuss the plot, develop the characters, and mold the themes for their latest book, *A Yellow Raft in Blue Water*.

For Erdrich and Dorris, their novels are very much the offspring of their marriage. In fact, Dorris once remarked that he and Erdrich become so involved in the conception of a character that they become like children. Both writers agree that the success of their novels can be attributed to the unique nature of their working relationship. As Dorris put it in the dedication to *A Yellow Raft in Blue Water*, Erdrich and he are "companions through every page." Indeed, it is hard to imagine a time when they were not together, but there was such a time.

◆ ◆ ◆

Michael Anthony Dorris was born on January 30, 1945, in Dayton, Washington. He was the son of James and Mary Dorris. James was a descendent of the Modoc, a tribe originally native to northern California and southern Oregon. From his parents, who used to tell him stories, Dorris developed an interest in literature. He read widely and wrote poems and stories. Also from his parents, Dorris seems to have inherited his restless nature and his love for travel. During his childhood, the family lived in Washington, Idaho, and Montana, all of which later became settings for his books. And in his adult life, Dorris has lived in many different places, including New Zealand and Alaska.

After graduating from high school, Dorris enrolled at Georgetown University in Washington, D.C., graduating from there in 1967 with a degree in English literature and classics. Dorris then returned to the West and became the director of the Urban Bus Program in Redlands, California. But this career was not to last. A year later he resumed his studies, this time at Yale University in New Haven, Connecticut. He completed a master's degree in the history of the theater at Yale in 1970. He then accepted a teaching position at Franconia College in New Hampshire, where he remained for the next two years. During this time, Dorris adopted three Native American children: Adam, Sava, and Madeleine. The mother of the eldest child, Adam, had recently died of alcohol poisoning. By 1972, Dorris's work in the area of Native American studies came to the attention of the faculty at Dartmouth College, a distinguished school that was originally created for the purpose of educating Indians. At Dartmouth, he was made an associate professor of anthropology and was put in charge of a fledgling program in Native American studies. That same year, Dartmouth opened its doors for the first time to women students. And the timing could not have been better. One member of this first class was a young woman of Chippewa descent named Louise Erdrich.

Erdrich was born on July 6, 1954 in Little Falls, Minnesota. She was the first of seven children born to Ralph Erdrich, a school-teacher employed by the Bureau of Indian Affairs, and Rita Erdrich, who also worked for the bureau. Like Dorris, Erdrich was of mixed blood. Her father was of German descent and her mother was a Turtle Mountain Chippewa. Both of her parents were avid readers and storytellers, and from them Erdrich developed an early interest in literature. As she recalled in an interview, her father would pay her a nickel for every story she wrote; her mother would then collect the stories and bind them together in card-board so that they made up a book. "At an early age," said Erdrich, "I felt myself to be a published author earning substantial royal-ties." This encouragement from her parents seems to have des-tined her for a career as a professional writer.

Unlike Dorris, Erdrich spent most of her youth in one place. Except for occasional visits to her grandparents, who lived on the Chippewa reservation, she grew up in Wahpeton, North Dakota, a small town situated on the Minnesota border to the south of Fargo, North Dakota. The tall, wind-blown grass, tilled beet fields, and wide open spaces surrounding this prairie town had a pow-erful effect on Erdrich's imagination. Both the landscape of this region and the small-town gossip characteristic of the community, which is like that of Prairie Lake and Argus in her fiction, helped to make her a writer. As she has said of herself and Dorris, "we both grew up in small communities where you were who you were in relation to the community." She attributes her sense of humor, however, to her occasional visits to the Chippewa reservation—"They have the best sense of humor of any group of people I've ever known." During these visits to her grandparents she also heard stories of the hardships faced by Native Americans during the depression era—stories that contributed to the writing of *The Beet Queen* in 1986.

Writing seems to have come naturally to Erdrich. While she was growing up, she kept a running account of her feelings and observations about life in a diary, which she claims was endlessly self-absorbed. Still, it helped her to develop the graceful and economical style that has been praised by critics. Like another great Native American writer, N. Scott Momaday, she also came to admire the writing of William Faulkner, especially his technique of telling a story from the point of view of a number of different characters. In fact, all of her novels consist of a series of short stories told by various characters, thus giving many different perspectives on the Native American and mixed-blood experience.

Erdrich's interest in literature was encouraged by her parents and, because she lived on the campus of Wahpeton Indian School where her parents taught, she also grew up in a moderately scholarly environment. She attended public schools through the ninth grade, then attended St. John's Catholic School for three years. Erdrich's Catholicism and her experiences at parochial school later provided the material for her second book of poetry, *Baptism of Fire*, a book which also reveals her fascination with Christian saints and martyrs.

During her formative years, Erdrich also developed an interest in the visual arts, which competed with poetry and fiction as a means of expressing her feelings. In fact, when she applied to Dartmouth College in 1972, she had not decided on a course of study. Her first love was writing, however, and she worked at it with even greater enthusiasm after taking a course in Native American studies at Dartmouth. The instructor was Michael Dorris. Before taking Dorris's course, Erdrich says she had never thought of drawing on her Chippewa heritage or of writing about small-town life in North Dakota. She was impressed particularly by the emphasis and importance Dorris assigned to Native

Michael Dorris's course in Native American studies at Dartmouth College encouraged Erdrich to write about her Chippewa heritage. (Photo by Louise Erdrich; Courtesy of Henry Holt and Company)

American life and culture. Since that time, for Erdrich the lives of Native Americans and mixed-bloods in a small North Dakota town have been a rich source of fictional material.

In 1973, Dorris left Dartmouth for a job as visiting professor at the University of New Hampshire and became the chairman of the Native American Council, a position that he has held off and on ever since. In that same year, the tireless Dorris served as a consultant to the National Endowment for the Humanities. He returned to Dartmouth for the academic year 1975–76, the year in which Erdrich enrolled in his course.

Erdrich completed her degree in English and creative writing in 1976. By this time she had already won a number of undergraduate prizes for her poetry and stories, including the Academy of American Poets Prize for student poetry. In the summer of 1976, she worked for a small press distribution company in Boston. Determined to make writing her career, however, Erdrich applied and was accepted into the Johns Hopkins University graduate writing program in Baltimore, Maryland. At Johns Hopkins, Erdrich took workshops in writing poetry and short stories. According to Erdrich, her writing evolved from the shorter medium of poetry to the writing of short stories, and only later did she conceive of the idea of connecting a series of stories to form a novel.

Erdrich graduated from Johns Hopkins with a master of fine arts degree in 1977 and, because she was not yet able to earn enough money from her writing, she was forced to look for alternate means of support. She was able to find work in the visual arts, formerly her main interest, and assisted in the making of a film for the Mid-American Television Company on the conflict between the Sioux and Eastern European settlers in the 1800s. After this project was completed, she was hired by the National Endowment for the Arts, who had started a poetry-in-the-schools program. This job gave Erdrich a chance to return home to North Dakota, where she toured a number of different schools teaching poetry to children. But as Erdrich was later to admit, she was not temperamentally suited to teaching. (In an interview, she remarked that she was not a very good teacher, while Dorris, on the other hand, was the greatest teacher in the world.)

During her free time, Erdrich continued to write, and her stories and poems increasingly began to appear in top literary journals.

She also completed her first novel, titled *Tracks,* but could not find a publisher. In 1979, just as Erdrich was beginning to be recognized by the literary establishment, she returned to her alma mater, Dartmouth, for a brief visit. During this visit, Erdrich became reacquainted with her former professor, Michael Dorris, who had taken an interest in her development as a writer. Although Dorris was about to travel halfway across the globe for a year of teaching and research at the University of Auckland in New Zealand, the two decided to stay in touch. They continued to write to each other over the next year, commenting and offering advice on each other's work. This correspondence, evidently, became more frequent and more intimate. In 1981, they were married.

The couple then moved into an old farmhouse in New Hampshire and, combining their considerable writing abilities, got down to the business of writing. Although Dorris kept his teaching post at Dartmouth, he became Erdrich's editor, advisor, and literary agent. In addition to Erdrich's own work, the two began to collaborate, publishing stories in *Redbook* and *Women* magazines under the name of Milou North. Erdrich and Dorris cleverly combined their first names to make "Milou," and added the surname "North" because, as Dorris remarked, "it sounded literary."

Fame and success did not come, however, until a few years later, in 1984. This year, which was also the year in which their first biological child, Persia, was born, was momentous for the couple. Erdrich published both her first book of poetry, *Jacklight,* and her first novel, *Love Medicine. Love Medicine,* a collection of linked stories that chronicle the troubled lives of three generations of a family, drew on Erdrich's experiences growing up among Native Americans, mixed-bloods, and non-Indians in Wahpeton. This novel revealed Erdrich's interest in the subject of the experience of mixed-blood Native Americans and their feeling of belonging neither to Native American nor to white American culture—of being always outsiders. The novel was an instant success; it was praised by critics, climbed the best-seller list, and received a number of literary awards, including the prestigious National Book Critics' award for the best novel of 1984. *Jacklight,* although it did not sell as well as *Love Medicine,* was named one

Louise Erdrich's first novel, Love Medicine *(1984), brought her immediate acclaim and placed her among the writers of the Native American literary renaissance.* (Photo by Michael Dorris; Courtesy of HarperCollins)

of the 10 best books of poetry for 1984 by the *San Francisco Chronicle.*

The novel was credited to Erdrich, but Dorris played a key part in its composition. In fact, Erdrich's and Dorris's books, regardless of whose name appears on the cover, are always very much a collaborative effort. The two begin by discussing an idea for a story, a plot or an observation. After pondering this idea over a period of time, either Erdrich or Dorris will write up a draft of the plot. Then they will discuss the plot further, making revisions and changes. They repeat this process five or six times more as the details of plot and characterization become more specific. Then the characters are developed and visualized so that both writers can conceive of them as real people. Part of the success of Erdrich's novels is due to the authenticity of her characters and the way their personality is revealed through first-person narrative. An example of such a character is Mary Adare in *The Beet Queen*, who not only has well-defined physical features but is able to describe these herself with insight and honesty.

Once the discussion is complete and both Dorris and Erdrich feel comfortable with the draft, the writing begins. Ultimately, no book goes to press without each agreeing on nearly every sentence. Erdrich and Dorris say that they trust each other's judgment completely. In the case of Erdrich and Dorris, two heads really are better than one.

As Erdrich has said, her marriage to Dorris has made her much more efficient and productive in her own writing. She has re-marked that, when she first married Dorris, she could not believe how busy he was. She kept thinking that it would eventually stop and that they would lead a more settled life. Now she has come to accept that such "busy-ness" is in the nature of their life together. The couple's list of accomplishments bears this out. Throughout the 1980s, Dorris continued to conduct field work in anthropology, to lecture, and to serve as chairman of the Native American Council. In addition, he has been closely involved in the study of Native American literature, writing a number of introductions to books by and about Native Americans, and publishing articles on the study of the Native American literary tradition. His hard work, indeed, seems to have rubbed off on Erdrich, who began planning a series of three novels to continue the story begun in *Love Medicine*. Her second novel, *The Beet Queen*, did not disappoint the expectations of readers and critics, and it became a best-seller in 1986.

That same year, 1986, saw the couple traveling to Northridge, Minnesota so that Dorris could do research for a book about fetal alcohol syndrome among Sioux Indians at the Pine Ridge reservation in South Dakota. Dorris saw this work as one of the most important things that he could do for his fellow Native Americans, among whom alcoholism and birth defects resulting from alcoholism are serious problems. The fruit of Dorris's extensive work at Pine Ridge was *The Broken Cord,* which appeared in 1989. The book brought wide attention to the problem of fetal alcohol syndrome (called FAS for short) and suggested ways in which it might be prevented. In many ways, it was Dorris's way of giving something valuable to Native Americans, whose history is tragically associated with alcohol abuse. Many times throughout their sad history since the coming of Europeans, Native Americans have signed away land, neglected their farming, and even died through the abuse of alcohol. This subject is one that is very close to Dorris's heart, for his adopted son Adam suffers from FAS. *The Broken Cord* is stirring in the way that it combines social research and personal experience in a discussion of the terrible effects of FAS and the ways in which it ruins a child's chances at living a full life.

The temporary move to Minnesota, with its landscape of the plains and its nearness to the Dakotas, helped to revive Erdrich's creative energies, which she confessed had gone through a bit of a drought after the publication of *The Beet Queen.* Taking her husband's advice, she returned to the manuscript of her first novel and began rewriting the book. The result was *Tracks,* a novel that deals with the thoughts and feelings of the Chippewa as they see their traditional life and culture begin to disappear in the early years of the 20th century. *Tracks* also presents a realistic picture of the corrupt practices of federal and tribal officials, who often cheated Native Americans out of land and money.

Tracks was, not surprisingly, dedicated to Dorris, "whose presence, of course, is inextricable from this story." The presence of Dorris in Erdrich's work and of Erdrich in Dorris's work goes without saying. The chance meeting and eventual marriage of the couple has proved to be fortunate, both for them, for the reading public, and for contemporary Native American literature. Perhaps the ultimate achievement for Dorris and Erdrich came in 1991 with the publication of the novel *The Crown of Columbus.* For the first time, Erdrich's and Dorris's names appeared together on the cover of a novel. *The Crown of Columbus,* an ambitious examination of how Columbus's arrival in the Americas affected Native American life, was a testament to the success of their partnership. How did Dorris and Erdrich come up with the idea for this book? Well, they were driving across the seemingly endless grassy plain from Saskatchewan to Manitoba, Canada. . . .

Today Erdrich and Dorris remain active in issues concerning Native Americans, including fetal alcohol syndrome, Indian rights, and land restoration. Dorris, true to his nature, has been especially busy. In 1991 he published *Morning Girl,* a children's book about a brother and sister who witness the colonization of a Bahamian island by members of Columbus's party in 1492, and how they come to the realization that their old way of life is gone forever. In the summer of 1992, Dorris served as a board member of the Save the Children Fund and visited refugee camps in Zimbabwe, Africa. His experiences there among the Tonga tribe and their struggles with famine and drought are recorded in *Rooms in the House of Stone,* which was published in October of 1993. During this period, Dorris also found time to write another novel, *Working Men,* published in June 1993. Although not as prolific as her husband, Erdrich has completed the much-anticipated final novel in her four-novel series—a work called *Bingo Palace.* In addition, she has revised and added five sections to *Love Medicine,* her much-heralded first novel, for republication.

Erdrich and Dorris currently live, write, and raise their children in Kalispell, Montana.

SELECTED BIBLIOGRAPHY

◆ ◆ ◆

Books on Native American Literature

Coltelli, Laura. *Winged Words: American Indian Writers Speak.* Lincoln, NE: University of Nebraska Press, 1990. A collection of interviews designed by the author to allow contemporary American Indian writers to discuss their own cultural heritage and its place in their work. Coltelli interviews such major figures as N. Scott Momaday, Paula Gunn Allen, Joy Harjo, Louise Erdrich, and Michael Dorris.

Lincoln, Kenneth. *Native American Renaissance.* Berkeley: University of California Press, 1983. A study of contemporary Native American writers in the context of their tribal culture and its particular oral literary tradition. Includes studies of N. Scott Momaday, James Welch, and Leslie Marmon Silko. May be too advanced for young readers.

Ruoff, A. LaVonne Brown. *American Indian Literatures: An Introduction, Bibliographic Review, and Selected Bibliography.* New York: Modern Language Association, 1990. A highly useful guide to the study of American Indian literature—a history of both the oral and written literature, a survey of criticism, and a record of publications.

———. *Literature of the American Indian.* New York: Chelsea House, 1991. An illustrated young adult book on the subject.

Anthologies of Native American Literature

Green, Rayna, ed. *That's What She Said: Contemporary Poetry and Fiction by Native American Women.* Bloomington, IN: Indiana University Press, 1984. An anthology of writing that includes the work of such important authors as Paula Gunn Allen, Joy Harjo, Louise Erdrich, Mary Tallmountain, and Wendy Rose.

Lerner, Andrea, ed. *Dancing on the Rim of the World: An Anthology of Contemporary Northwest Native American Writing.* Tucson: University of Arizona Press, 1990. This anthology includes works by poets Jim Barnes, James Welch, and Mary Tallmountain.

Niatum, Duane, ed. *Harper's Anthology of 20th Century Native American Poetry*. New York: Harper, 1988. Perhaps the most complete presentation of verse written by Native Americans in this century. Includes poems by N. Scott Momaday, Jim Barnes, Joy Harjo, James Welch, and Louise Erdrich.

Peyer, Bernard C., ed. *The Singing Spirit: Early Short Stories by North American Indians*. Tucson: University of Arizona Press, 1989. This anthology includes stories by Native American writers of the late 19th and early 20th centuries, including Charles Eastman, Alexander Posey, Francis La Flesche, Susette La Flesche, and John Joseph Mathews.

Rothenberg, Jerome, ed. *Shaking the Pumpkin: Traditional Poetry of the Indian North Americas*. Garden City, NY: Doubleday, 1972. This anthology contains a wide variety of poetry written by Native Americans in their own language and freely translated into English.

About Sequoyah

Carter, Samuel III. *Cherokee Sunset: A Nation Betrayed*. New York: Doubleday, 1976. A general history of the Cherokee, beginning with their alliance with the United States in the war against the Creek and concluding with their resettlement in the West. Includes a discussion of the assassinations of Major and John Ridge, the Trail of Tears, and the invention of Sequoyah's syllabary.

Coblentz, Catherine Kate. *Sequoyah*. New York: Longmans, Green, 1946. Presents Sequoyah's life and work against the background of Cherokee history. Reads like a novel for young adults, and the facts and events of Sequoyah's life are filled in by the author's colorful descriptions.

Cwiklik, Robert. *Sequoyah*. Englewood, NJ: Silver Burdett Press, 1989. A full-length biography of Sequoyah written for young adults.

Frederick, Jack, and Anna Gritts Kilpatrick, trans. and ed. *The Shadow of Sequoyah: Social Documents of the Cherokees, 1862–1964*. Norman, OK: University of Oklahoma Press, 1965. Traces the uses and development of the Cherokee language since the invention of Sequoyah's syllabary. The documents included range from an account of a smallpox epidemic and love incantations to the letters of a medicine man.

By and About John Rollin Ridge

Parins, James W. *John Rollin Ridge: His Life and Works.* Lincoln, NE: University of Nebraska Press, 1991. The definitive biography of the Cherokee journalist, novelist, and poet. Includes an excellent account of his father's and grandfather's assassinations, his experiences during the Gold Rush, and his involvement in the newspaper wars in California in the 1850s.

Ridge, John Rollin. *The Life and Adventures of Joaquin Murieta, the Celebrated California Bandit.* Norman, OK: University of Oklahoma Press, 1986. Still in print in paperback, this sensational and highly entertaining book captures the spirit embodied in the legend of the famous California outlaw.

Wilkins, Thurman. *Cherokee Tragedy: The Story of the Ridge Family and of the Decimation of a People.* London: Collier, 1970. A focused study of the Ridge family, the rivalry that existed between the Ridges and John Ross, the assassinations of Major and John Ridge, and the events leading up to Cherokee removal and the Trail of Tears.

By and About Sarah Winnemucca

Canfield, Gae Whitney. *Sarah Winnemucca of the Northern Paiutes.* Norman, OK: University of Oklahoma Press, 1983. A thorough, sympathetic biography set against the backdrop of the struggle of the Paiute to retain their traditional homeland, with a focus on Sarah Winnemucca's role in the struggle.

Knack, Martha C., and Omer C. Stewart. *As Long as the River Shall Run: An Ethnohistory of Pyramid Lake Indian Reservation.* Berkeley: University of California Press, 1984. A scholarly account of the struggles of the Paiute at Pyramid Lake against the abuses of agency officials. Contains a brief examination of Sarah Winnemucca's role in these events and her importance in Paiute history. May be too difficult for young readers.

Scordato, Ellen. *Sarah Winnemuca.* New York: Chelsea House, 1991. A very detailed account of Winnemucca's life for young readers, illustrated with period photos.

Winnemucca, Sarah. *Life Among the Piutes: Their Wrongs and Claims.*

Reprint. Bishop, CA: Chalfant Press, 1969. Winnemucca's autobiographical account of the struggles of her people, their mistreatment by U.S. agency officials, and her protest against government Indian policy.

By and About Susette, Francis, and Susan La Flesche

Brown, Marion M. *Susette La Flesche: Advocate for Native American Rights*. Chicago: Children's Press, 1991. Covers La Flesche for young adults. Gives cultural context but provides a somewhat superficial treatment of the subject.

Clarke, Dorothy Wilson. *Bright Eyes: The Story of Susette La Flesche*. New York: McGraw-Hill, 1974. A very entertaining rendition of Susette's life, complete with accounts of Omaha ceremonies, imaginative dialogue, and colorful description. Although *Bright Eyes* is a long book, it is excellent for young readers.

Fletcher, Alice, and Francis La Flesche. *The Omaha Tribe*. New York: Johnson Reprint Co., 1980. This monumental study and record of Omaha culture was the result of nearly 20 years of work by Fletcher and La Flesche. It includes detailed descriptions of Omaha tribal organization, government, music, warfare, religion, and burial rites.

Green, Norma Kidd. *Iron Eye's Family: The Children of Joseph LaFlesche*. Lincoln, NE: Johnson Publishing Co., 1969. Tells the story of the last chief of the Omaha and his multitalented offspring, Susette, Francis, and Susan. Also gives an interesting account of the situation of a man caught between the traditional ways of his people and the need to adapt to the non-Indian world.

La Flesche, Francis. *The Middle Five: Indian Schoolboys of the Omaha Tribe*. Lincoln, NE: University of Nebraska Press, 1978. This is La Flesche's memoir of his childhood years spent in a Presbyterian mission school on the Omaha reservation. It presents a series of portraits of his friends and fondly recalls incidents, some humorous and some serious, from his school days. This book offers young readers a rare glimpse of Indian boyhood and of being "caught between two worlds."

———. "The Osage Tribe." In *36th Annual Report of the Bureau of American Ethnology*. Washington, D.C.: Government Printing

Office, 1921. Presents the research La Flesche did on the Osage for the Bureau of American Ethnology during the years 1915–16. Includes a study of Osage language and tribal rites, and provides English translations of many ceremonial songs.

Liberty, Margot. "Francis La Flesche, Omaha, 1857–1932." In *American Indian Intellectuals*, ed. Margot Liberty. St. Paul: West Publishing, 1978. This article provides a brief overview of Francis's life and work. The author focuses on Francis's professional life and assesses his contribution to Native American anthropology.

Mattes, Valerie Sherer. "Dr. Susan La Flesche Picotte: The Reformed and the Reformer." In *Indian Lives: Essays on Nineteenth- and Twentieth-Century Native American Leaders*, ed. L. G. Moses and Raymond Wilson. Albuquerque: University of New Mexico Press, 1985. This essay provides a brief overview of Dr. La Flesche's career, her struggles to become the first Native American woman physician, and her work among the Omaha.

By and About Charles A. Eastman

Copeland, Marion. *Charles Alexander Eastman (Ohiyesa)*. Boise, ID: Boise State University Press, 1978. A brief but useful survey and analysis of Eastman's writings.

Eastman, Charles. *From the Deep Woods to Civilization*. Lincoln, NE: University of Nebraska Press, 1977. This book is the follow-up to *Indian Boyhood*. It narrates Eastman's experiences and struggles in trying to assimilate into the non-Indian world, from first learning to read in English and his conversion to Christianity, to medical school. Eastman concludes with his thoughts and impressions on Wounded Knee, the Ghost Dance War, and the spiritual differences between the Indian and non-Indian worlds.

———. *Indian Boyhood*. New York: Dover, 1971. This book, Eastman's first, was written for his children. It tells of his early childhood in Canada and of the traditional ways of the Sioux.

———. *Indian Heroes and Great Chieftains*. Lincoln, NE: University of Nebraska Press, 1991. Contains Eastman's biographical portraits of famous Native American leaders, some of whom were Eastman's personal friends. Among the figures discussed are

Crazy Horse, Red Cloud, Sitting Bull, and Chief Joseph.

Graber, Kay, ed. *Sister to the Sioux: The Memoirs of Elaine Goodale Eastman, 1885–1891.* Lincoln, NE: University of Nebraska Press, 1978. In this memoir, the wife of Charles Eastman tells the story of her experience of leaving a wealthy, privileged position in the East to become a teacher on a Sioux reservation. The memoir concludes with her impressions of Wounded Knee and her subsequent marriage to Eastman.

Wilson, Raymond. *Ohiyesa: Charles Eastman: Santee Sioux.* Urbana, IL: University of Illinois Press, 1983. The definitive biography of Eastman. Tells the story of Eastman's personal struggles, his assimilation into non-Indian society, his marital relationship with Elaine Goodale, and his work as a doctor, writer, and businessman.

By and About Alexander Posey

Littlefield, Daniel F., Jr. *Alex Posey: Creek Poet, Journalist and Humorist.* Lincoln, NE: University of Nebraska Press, 1992. This biography of the great Creek man of letters tells the story of a tremendous talent, his rise from poverty and subsequent success in business, and his tragic early death.

Posey, Alexander. *The Fus Fixico Letters.* Lincoln, NE: University of Nebraska Press, 1993. This volume collects for the first time the fictional letters that represent Posey's major literary achievement.

By and About James R. Murie

Dorsey, George A. *The Pawnee.* Washington, D.C.: Carnegie Institute, 1906. This book collects some 140 Pawnee medicine ceremonies, tales, and religious myths that Dorsey translated with the help of James R. Murie, the Pawnee ethnologist.

Murie, James R. *Ceremonies of the Pawnee,* ed. Douglas R. Parks. Lincoln, NE: University of Nebraska Press, 1989. This book, the only work by Murie still in print, represents the first of Murie's studies resumed after the completion of George Dorsey's *The Pawnee.* This is one of the most extensive studies of ceremonies and songs ever done on a Native American people.

Parks, Douglas R. "James R. Murie: Pawnee Ethnographer." In *American Indian Intellectuals,* ed. Margot Liberty. St. Paul: West Publishing, 1978. A brief but excellent overview of Murie's life and work, written by the editor of Murie's *Ceremonies of the Pawnee.*

About Jesse Cornplanter

Fenton, William H. (Howã' ñeyeo, the Hawk). "'Aboriginally Yours,' Jesse J. Cornplanter, Hah-Yonh-Wonh-Ish, The Snipe." In *American Indian Intellectuals,* ed. Margot Liberty. St. Paul: West Publishing, 1978. This rendering of Cornplanter's life, written by a longtime friend and distinguished anthropologist, offers an intimate as well as scholarly estimation of the man's achievements.

By John Joseph Mathews

Mathews, John Joseph. *The Osage: Children of the Middle Waters.* Norman, OK: University of Oklahoma Press, 1961. Mathews's monumental history of his people from pre-European times to the 20th century. Includes excellent descriptions of Osage ceremonies, religious rites, and myths. Mathews's style of historical writing is unique in that a large part of his information comes from Osage oral tradition as told to him by tribal elders and is colored by fiction and myth.

————. *Wa'Kon-Tah: The Osage and the White Man's Road.* Norman, OK: University of Oklahoma Press, 1932. Mathews's fictional rendition of the Osage's struggles to retain their traditional lifestyle in the face of the intervention of the non-Indian world in the mid-19th century. Based on the journals of Major Laban J. Miles, the first government agent to the Osage tribe.

By and About N. Scott Momaday

Momaday, N. Scott. *House Made of Dawn.* New York: Harper & Row, 1969. The novel for which Momaday was awarded the Pulitzer Prize. A difficult but moving story of an Indian's struggle to come to grips with his ethnicity amid the confusion of the post–World War II era.

————. *In the Presence of the Sun*. New York: St. Martin's, 1992. A collection of Momaday's best poetry, both selected and new. The paintings and drawings, also by Momaday, placed beside the poems, make this a unique volume.

————. *The Way to Rainy Mountain*. Albuquerque: University of New Mexico Press, 1969. An excellent introduction to Kiowa myths and legends for young readers. Also contains illustrations by Momaday's father, Alfred.

Schubnell, Mathias. *N. Scott Momaday: The Cultural and Literary Background*. A critical survey of Momaday's fiction and poetry up until *The Names*. Also includes a brief biographical essay and a study of Yvor Winters's influence on Momaday's writing.

Woodard, Charles L. *Ancestral Voices: Conversations with N. Scott Momaday*. Contains a series of interviews the author conducted with the Kiowa writer in 1986 and 1987. Also includes 29 reproductions of Momaday's paintings.

By and About Michael Dorris and Louise Erdrich

Dorris, Michael. *The Broken Cord*. New York: HarperCollins, 1992. An autobiographical account of Dorris's adopted son and their shared struggle with fetal alcohol syndrome.

————. *Morning Girl*. New York: Hyperion, 1992. A children's book. The sad but compelling story of two Bahamian island children who witness the arrival of Columbus in 1492.

————. *A Yellow Raft in Blue Water*. New York: Holt, Rinehart and Winston, 1987. This book for young adults tells the story of three generations of hardy Indian women who are joined by bonds of kinship. The tale takes place in Seattle and on a Montana reservation.

Erdrich, Louise. *The Beet Queen*. New York: Henry Holt, 1986. This novel continues the story of some of the characters who were first introduced in *Love Medicine*.

————. *Jacklight*. New York: Henry Holt, 1984. This, Erdrich's first book of poems, shows her concern for her family and for her Chippewa mixed-blood lineage. The title derives from a Chippewa word that can mean either "hunting" or "flirting."

————. *Love Medicine*. New York: Henry Holt, 1984. This, Erdrich's first novel, set the standard for her lyrical and deceptively simple style. Here begins the story of an extended North Dakota family as told by a number of different narrators. *Love Medicine* can be read as a collection of short stories or as a continuous narrative.

George, Jan. "Interview with Louise Erdrich." *North Dakota Quarterly*, Spring 1985. In this interview, conducted shortly after the success of *Love Medicine*, Erdrich discusses her background, how she came to write her first novel, and her first book of poetry, *Jacklight*.

Schumacher, Michael. "Louise Erdrich and Michael Dorris: A Marriage of Minds." *Writer's Digest*, June 1, 1991. In this interview, Erdrich and Dorris reveal the true nature of their working relationship and their writing processes.

Wong, Hertha D. "An Interview with Louise Erdrich and Michael Dorris." *North Dakota Quarterly*, Winter 1987. In this lighthearted dialogue, Erdrich and Dorris discuss their respective backgrounds and the projects on which they are currently working.

INDEX

Boldface type indicates main headings.
Italic type indicates illustrations.

◆ ◆ ◆